My Montana

by Nadine Ann Shirley

RoseDog❖Books
PITTSBURGH, PENNSYLVANIA 15238

RoseDog Books
585 Alpha Drive, Suite 103
Pittsburgh, PA 15238
Visit our website at *www.rosedogbookstore.com*

ISBN: 979-8-88729-435-3
eISBN: 979-8-88729-935-8

DEDICATION

This book is dedicated to:

My parents and sisters who introduced me to Montana and without whom I never would have had the privilege;

The Class of 1958 from Billings Senior High School with whom I grew up and became a Montanan;

My former husband and our children from whom I learned many wonderful things about life from another's perspective but always with "My Montana" values as a sanctuary; and

Any human being on the planet who has had any relationship at all with Montana, because that means you have been blessed. Montana is a special place, according to Abraham Lincoln a "perfect" place. Enjoy it and share it.

ACKNOWLEDGMENTS

A great big Thank You to all those who contributed their comments to "My Montana:"   (in order of appearance in the book)

Greg Smith	John and Shirley Cadby
Katie Seibel	Matt Campbell
Shirley Cadby	Mike Campbell
Sue Zimmerman	Agnes Cowan
Toby and Robin (Cadby)	Georgette Scheafer
Sorensen	Doris Madison
Dick Ford	Frances Haley
Mitch Campbell	Clara Borland
Mason Campbell	Kori Campbell
Frank Jarvenpaa	Kellie Campbell-Cozart

And a Greater and Bigger Thank You to Robin Cadby Sorensen for the many hours she spent editing all three of my books – *On Being Old, People are Messy and They Leak*, and *My Montana.*

TABLE OF CONTENTS

"I'm in love with Montana. For other states I have admiration, respect, recognition, even some affection. But with Montana, it is love. And it's difficult to analyze love when you're in it."

— *by John Steinbeck*

INTRODUCTION

Montana is my home. I was born and grew up in **Billings**, the largest city in the state. (Population is roughly 150,000 now but was closer to 55,000 in my day.) I graduated from Billings Senior High School and babies one, two, five and six were born at St. Vincent's Hospital (now SCL Health), as was I. Excluding a brief two-year side trip to Colorado (where baby number four was born at Lutheran Hospital), I lived in Montana until age 35 when I moved with my then husband and children to California.

I lived in **Bozeman** for almost a year, while my then husband was attending Montana State College (which is now Montana State University). We lived in student housing that consisted of old Army barracks with little or no insulation. In a country where the snow piles up and the temperature goes down, this does not provide comfortable living conditions. And we were there with our two, very young children. I worked in the Education Department as secretary to the Dean of Undergraduate Studies, walking to and from work in, very often, very deep snow. I'm sure Bozeman has always had good skiing areas because there is a ton of snow in Bozeman. It snowed the August day we moved in and the June day we moved out. When I lived there, Bozeman was a small agricultural town with no other claim to fame than the land grant college it housed. (Land grant colleges were established to promote education in agricultural and mechanical arts/engineering.)

I lived in **Missoula** for roughly four years, in two different time frames, each under very different, yet similar circumstances. The first two years were while my then husband (the same then husband with whom I lived in Billings and Bozeman) was completing his bachelor's degree at the University of Montana. We again lived in student housing but new buildings that were built for that purpose. We had the same two small children and added baby number three before we left, born at St. Patrick's Hospital. Missoula was a small logging and paper mill town with periods of time that the stench in the air coming from those mills was barely tolerable.

I lived in **Big Fork**, which sits on the edge of Flathead Lake, the biggest fresh water lake west of the Mississippi, for probably three years, although I owned the property on Woods Bay for a few years longer. By now I was divorced, no longer had children for whom I was responsible and had acquired two little dogs, Bichons named Sugar and Kream. At that time, Big Fork was a very small community that, for the most part, was only functional during the summer months. There was a live, repertoire theater that was the centerpiece of all activities. The construction and expansion that has resulted in the current, commercially attractive Big Fork, began when I was living there in the early 1990's.

The second two-year stint in **Missoula** followed my time in Big Fork and was thirty years later than the first, when I, myself, was completing my bachelor's degree at the University. I was able to rent a relatively new apartment, that was not real close to campus, but close enough. The town had grown up some since my previous time there, but was still primarily a university town with students dominating the landscape and the calendar of events. That corresponded nicely with my focus while there. And I don't recall any of the paper mill stench from earlier days.

I lived in **Columbus** for six years following my retirement, in a mother-in-law's apartment in my daughter's home. My number five child and youngest daughter Kori, and her husband Matt, own a restaurant in which I was the Chairman in Charge of Silverware Wrapping. Columbus is unique in appearance because the main street is one-sided, meaning there are buildings along one side but only a railroad track and empty ground along the other side. That was always a bit off-putting to me.

And finally, I have been living in **Nye** since 2020, when my number one child and oldest daughter, Kellie, who lives in California, and I purchased a cabin on the Stillwater River. Nye is in the very small category of communities in Montana and certainly the smallest in which I have ever lived. Nye covers a large swath of land, approximately 226 square miles, because they estimate one person per square mile and according to the 2020 census there are 226 people living in Nye. I am only acquainted with maybe 30 in my sub-community in the Midnight Canyon. I am 35 minutes from Columbus and another 35 from Billings, which makes a round trip a good two and one-half hours, meaning trips to Billings, and any significant shopping, require planning. Today is October 12, 2021, and I am looking at approximately 14 inches of snow that has fallen in the last 24 hours. That is another factor that has polished my planning skills. Oh, and one more thing, both of my dogs (a second pair of Bichons, Koko and Kasper) have been attacked by very aggressive female deer, one almost to his death. Whew! Ask me why I love living here.

Taken on 10/12/21 in my back yard.

So, my point is: I have lived in Montana a total of 47 out of my 81 years of life. Not to mention that every year that I was not living here I came to visit for two to four weeks on vacation, bringing as many children as possible with me. My parents and sister lived in Montana until their deaths, and I still have one sister and her children living here. My father and grandfather built a six-sided cabin just one cabin away from my current home.

But, having said all that, there is much of Montana that I have never seen. Many town names are foreign to me. So, after a very brief conversation with my niece, Holli, and her husband, Frank, a decision was made to travel the state this summer in their recently purchased motor home. From the beginning, the plan was to see the popular sights that Montana has to offer, as well as traveling the secondary roads to cover some of the less notable venues. Montana is made up of small towns. With Billings being the largest, as already mentioned at maybe 150,000, and Ismay, being the smallest at 19 residents, with roughly 334 municipalities in between (129 Incorporated and 205 unincorporated), they could all be considered small.

What follows is "Travels with Nadine and Holli and Frank and Dione," my 88 year old sister, and Holli's mother, who was seriously ill with Covid-19 and is now very much recovered, physically. At the very least, I hope you enjoy your tour of Montana with us and at the most, I hope you find Montana a place you would like to see for yourself or, if you don't already, maybe even decide to live here.

*"My favorite state has not yet been invented. It
will be called Montana, and it will be perfect."*
—by Abraham Lincoln, 1864

BRIEF MONTANA HISTORY

The portion of Montana east of the Continental Divide was part of the Louisiana Purchase of 1803. As such, it was traversed by the members of the Lewis and Clark Expedition, aka the Corps of Discovery, thus leaving us with the historic Lewis and Clark Trail. President Thomas Jefferson was hoping to find a water route connecting the Missouri and Columbia rivers which would then connect the Pacific Ocean with the Mississippi River system, thus giving the new western land access to port markets out of the Gulf of Mexico and to eastern cities along the Ohio River and its minor tributaries. Jefferson's choice to lead the exploration was Meriwether Lewis, his former secretary and a fellow native of Albemarle County, Virginia. Having reached the rank of captain in the U.S. Army, Lewis possessed military discipline and experience that would prove invaluable. While in the Army, Lewis had served in a rifle company commanded by William Clark. It was Clark whom Lewis chose to assist him in leading the expedition. On February 28, 1803, Congress appropriated funds for the Expedition, and Jefferson's dream came closer to becoming a reality.

Meriwether Lewis and William Clark began their mission in May of 1804 by launching their boats into the Missouri River at St. Louis, Missouri. It ended on the south side of the Columbia River in December of 1805 (15 miles north of Seaside, Oregon). In between was their journey through Montana, starting at the North Dakota border, following the Missouri River to its headwaters at Three Forks, Montana. Then they followed the Jefferson River westward to the doorstep of the Shoshone Indian tribe (pronounced show-SHOW-nee), who were skilled at "traversing the great rock mountains with horses". Once over the Bitterroot Mountains, the Corps of Discovery shaped canoe-like vessels that transported them swiftly downriver to the mouth of the Columbia, where they wintered (1805-1806) at Fort Clatsop, on the present-day Oregon side of the river. Lewis and Clark were in Montana from April 29, 1805 to August 12, 1805 and again from the beginning of April 1806 to the end of August. On the return portion of the trip Lewis and his group took a northern route, Clark with Sacagawea (also spelled Sacajawea) and their group stayed to the south and they all met up at the mouth of the Yellowstone River on the Montana – North Dakota border. At the completion of their trip they were able to provide President Jefferson with maps of uncharted land, rivers, and mountains, many of which they had given names.

President Abraham Lincoln created the Montana Territory on May 26, 1864, and appointed Sidney Edgerton (pronounced with a soft "g" as in George) as its first governor. Edgerton was a politician, lawyer, judge and teacher from Ohio. He was an alleged member of the infamous Montana Vigilantes and was reputedly one of its founders. The capital during Edgerton's tenure was at Bannack, which is now a "ghost town." The first territorial legislature divided Montana into nine counties: **Beaverhead, Chouteau, Deer Lodge, Edgerton, Gallatin, Jefferson, Madison, Missoula and Big Horn.** All nine counties exist to this day with altered boundaries, and one, Edgerton, had a name change to **Lewis and Clark.**

Thomas Francis Meagher (pronounced Mar) was an Irish nationalist who came to the United States in 1852; studied law, worked as a journalist, joined the U.S. Army at the beginning of the Civil War, and following the Civil War, was appointed Montana's Territorial Secretary of State by President Andrew Johnson, and served as acting territorial governor in 1867. During Meagher's tenure the capital was at Virginia City. **Meagher** County was created in 1867 by changing boundaries within Choteau and Gallatin Counties. (When I was traveling through the British Isles in 2013, I stepped out of my hotel room in Waterford, Ireland, to a statue of Mr. Meagher in his Civil War uniform. Following is an excerpt from the inscription on that statue: "...After the War Meagher became Secretary and Acting

Governor of the Montana Territory. He drowned in the Missouri River near Fort Benton on July 1, 1867....")

Montana was admitted to the union In November of 1889, along with North and South Dakota and Washington. By this time the capital had been moved to Helena, where it remains today. The first governor of the new state was Joseph K. Toole. He was a Democrat from Helena, a former territorial Legislator, and territorial delegate to the United States Congress. He was elected in 1889 and served until 1893, but because he was so popular he was re-elected to the post for two more terms from 1901 to 1908.

The 41st state, Montana lies south of Canada, west of North and South Dakota, north of Wyoming and east of Idaho. Montana shares 545 miles of border with Canada which include the provinces of Alberta, British Columbia and Saskatchewan. It is the fourth largest state by size at 145,546 square miles, following Alaska, Texas and California, in that order. California claims 155,959 square miles. The smallest state is Rhode Island with 1,034 square miles. When ranked by population, Montana is number 44 with 1,032,949 people which means a density of 7 people per square mile. Compare this to California with 39,144,818 people for a density of 251 people per square mile and Rhode Island with a population of 1,061,509 for a density of 1,027 people per square mile.

The Montana state flag was adopted in 1905, adding the word MONTANA above the seal in 1981 and specifying the font to be Helvetica Bold in 1985. The state seal in the center of the flag features an image of a landscape with plains, forests and mountains along the Great Falls at the Missouri River. There is a plow, shovel and pick located on the land, symbolizing the industries in the state. The territorial motto of "Oro y Plata" is found on a banner at the bottom of the seal. This is a Spanish phrase that means "Gold and Silver," which were found in abundance in Montana. The state name also came from Spanish. As the story goes, two Spanish colonizers named the territory Montana del Norte, meaning northern mountains.

"Montana" was adopted as the state song on February 20, 1945. It was written by Charles Cohan and composed by Joseph

E. Howard. I just discovered that it has several verses, but the chorus, which is all that I have ever known, is:

Montana. Montana. Glory of the west.
Of all the states from coast to coast you're easily the best.
Montana. Montana. Where skies are always blue.
M – O – N- T – A – N – A, Montana I love you.

The state nickname is Treasure State, state animal the Grizzly Bear, state bird the Meadowlark, state tree the Ponderosa Pine and state flower the Bitterroot.

Starting in 1933 Montana license plates were given a prefix number reflecting the county in which the vehicle was registered. Therefore, those prefix numbers had to be assigned to counties and it was decided that it would be done by population. The county with the most people was assigned the number one, which in 1933, according to the 1930 census, was Silver Bow County, the home of Butte, with 39,532 people. In second place with the number two was Cascade County, home of Great Falls, with a population of 28,822 people, and third with the number three was Yellowstone County, home of Billings, with 16,380 people. The least populous county, therefore sporting number 56, because by then Montana had 56 counties, was Lincoln County, home of Libby, with a population of 7,089 people. Needless to say, the population correlations with license plate numbers are no longer current but remain reflective of their populations in 1933. By paying attention to license plates as you travel through Montana, you get a little bit of history on the fronts and backs of the vehicles you encounter.

The most populous counties in 2021 are: Yellowstone, County Seat Billings, License Number 3, with 164,731 people; Gallatin, County Seat Bozeman, License Number 6, with 118,960 people; and Missoula, County Seat Missoula, License Number 4, with 117,922 people. And not to be overlooked, the least populated is Petroleum, County Seat Winnet, License Number 55, with 496 people.

"If you're lucky enough to live in Montana,
you're lucky enough."

— Author Unknown

EASTERN MONTANA TOUR

Day One:

Travel from Home to Hardin (95 Miles) Through Boyd, Joliet, Rockvale, Edgar, Pryor and St. Xavier

Interests: Three Brothers Restaurant – Meal with Greg

Battle of the Little Bighorn Museum

Travel to Ashland (81 Miles) Through Crow Agency, Busby and Lame Deer

Interests: St. Labre Mission

Camp near Ashland: Red Shale Campground or along 212 in dispersed camping 5 miles east of Ashland

Day Two:

Travel Ashland to Glendive (327 Miles) Through Broadus, Alzada, Ekalaka, Baker, Wibaux and Medicine rocks

Interests: Makoshika State Park and Museum

Dinosaur & Fossil Museum

Camp at Makoshika State Park (need reservations) (277 Miles) OR

Camp at Medicine Rock State Park (169 Miles)

Day Three:

Travel Glendive to Sidney (54 Miles)

    Interests: Bill and Susan Zimmerman – Lunch

Travel Sidney to Scobey (130 Miles) Through Culbertson, Froid, Medicine Lake, Antelope, Plentywood, Redstone, Flaxville and Madoc

    Interests: Pioneer Town

Camp in Scobey

Days Four and Five:

Travel Scobey to Fort Peck (100 Miles) Wolf Point, Frazer, Nashua and Park Grove

    Interests: Live Theater - "Complete History of America"

                  "Forever Plaid"

                  Interpretive Center and Museum

                  Possible Dam Tour (Under discussion at this time)

                  Possible Boat Tour of Lake

Camp at Fort Peck: Corps of Engineers Campground, recreation.gov

Day Six:

Travel Fort Peck to Near Malta (75 Miles) Through Glasgow, Hinsdale and Saco

    Interests: Sleeping Buffalo Resort Hot Springs

Camp at Sleeping Buffalo or Nelson Reservoir

Day Seven:

Travel Sleeping Buffalo to Roberts (259 Miles) Through Malta, Grass Range, Roundup, Billings, Laurel, Rockvale, Joliet and Boyd

    Interests: Bowdoin National Wildlife Refuge

                  Slight detour off hiwy 191 to Old Mission and Natural Bridge on Fort Belknap Indian Reservation

Roberts is about 58 miles from my cabin on the Stillwater River that is considered to be in Nye, Montana.

Roberts is the home for all three of the people with whom I was traveling, so we started from there. Roberts is an unincorporated town in Carbon County, 13 miles from Red Lodge and has a population of 298. It was originally a railroad station named Merritt. Old timers say the name Roberts came from one of the first baggage men on the train that came through there who endeared himself to everyone. Others say it was named for W. Minor Roberts, a chief engineer on the Northern Pacific Railway.

Towns between Roberts and Hardin:

Boyd is a wide spot in the road with a population of 64. It was named for a homesteader, John Boyd. Many of the farmers in the area are of Finnish descent and have log house steam baths similar to those found in Finland.

Joliet was the shipping point for the produce from the surrounding area. It was reportedly named by a Northern Pacific official for the town he came from, Joliet, Illinois. (Pronunciations a little different: Jah-lee-ett Montana and Joe-lee-ett Illinois.) Population 633.

Rockvale was settled in 1893 along the Northern Pacific tracks where Rock Creek drains into the North Fork River. Its name comes from its location in Rock Creek Valley. The post office closed in 1914. It is currently a bar and casino and some homes, but there is no population attributed to the Rockvale name. In the 1950's, when I was in high school, Rockvale was a place that high school kids went on Friday nights. It consisted of a gas station, bar and restaurant that had an outdoor dance floor and teenagers could buy beer. My former husband got a little rowdy there one night and got hit in the head by a local policeman's Billy Club. I, however, never had the Rockvale experience.

Edgar (pronounced with a hard "g" as in good) was named for Henry Edgar, one of the discoverers of gold in Montana. Alternatively, and according to one old-timer, the town was started by a man named Thornton because he wanted to have a town with no saloon in it and named it after his brother. Population is 148 and its claim to fame is a bar and grill that serves the best beef steaks around.

Pryor has a population of 539 and was named for Nathaniel Hale Pryor, a sergeant in the Lewis and Clark Expedition. Pryor is home to **Chief Plenty Coups State Park** (pronounced plenty coo), our first stop on this tour. Chief Plenty Coups was a leader of the Crow Indian Nation.

(There is more on him in the section about the Crow Reservation.) At the age of eleven he had a vision that told of his future and that of his tribe, the story of which can be viewed on YouTube. The vision led him to what is now Pryor and the place where he built the home that remains for public viewing. It is surrounded by cottonwood trees and possibly the most peaceful feeling I have ever experienced. In addition, there is a spring near the house on land that otherwise has no evidence of water.

Chief Plenty Coups' House in Pryor

St. Xavier has a population of 136. It was established by Father Prando, a Jesuit Missionary, and two companions who founded a mission there. The church is still in use. The mission's school, affiliated with the St. Labre Mission School in Ashland on the Northern Cheyenne Reservation, also continues to operate but is now called the Pretty Eagle School, after a famous Crow chief. (Francis Xavier, after whom the town was named, was a Spanish Jesuit who lived as a Roman Catholic missionary in the 1500s. He was one of the first seven members of the Jesuit order and travelled extensively, particularly in India, Southeast Asia, and Japan, to share his faith. He is the patron saint of Roman Catholic missions).

After driving what seemed like forever on a road that was under repair, it happened. Loud Bang. Wobble, wobble. Slow to a stop. A blowout, of one of the dual tires on the back of the motor home. It was about 4:30 in the afternoon of our first day, a few miles from Hardin. Miracle of miracles, we found a tire shop that would come to put on the spare and the next morning we could get four new tires put on. So, slight change of plans: overnight in Hardin, in the parking lot beside the tire store.

Hardin is about 115 miles from my cabin on the Stillwater River that is considered to be in Nye, Montana.

Hardin is a town of 3,818 people, approximately 53% of which are Native American, situated just outside the northern boundary of the Crow Indian Reservation. Hardin was incorporated in 1911 and was named for Samuel H. Hardin, a cattleman who leased acreage on the nearby reservation to graze his cattle, and a personal friend of C. H. Morrill, president of the Lincoln Land Company which purchased and platted the town site. Hardin is about 15 miles north of the site of the **Battle of the Little Bighorn,** formerly known as Custer's Last Stand, and a museum that provides a miniature re-enactment that helps us understand the dynamics of that battle. Basically, the Battle of the Little Bighorn marked the most decisive Native American victory and the worst U.S. Army defeat in the long Plains Indian War. On June 25, 1876, Chiefs Crazy Horse and Sitting Bull led the Lakota Sioux, Northern Cheyenne, and Arapaho Indians to annihilate Lt. Col. George Armstrong Custer and all his troops. The only survivor on the side of the United States was a severely wounded horse named Comanche. The Hardin Area Chamber of Commerce conducts the annual Little Big Horn Days festival in the 3rd weekend in June.

It just so happens that my sister, who was on the trip with us, owned the movie theater and video store in Hardin for 20+ years. She then sold it to her son Greg Smith and his wife Kerri. They ran the movie theater until the Covid-19 pandemic put them out of business, but by then they had added a restaurant, the Three Brothers, where we had dinner that first night, following a tire blow-out. Good food, pizza, and good company, hoping it to be an auspicious start to the trip. When I asked

Greg what it was like having a business in a town that is so close to an Indian reservation, he responded as follows: "There are challenges to be sure, but there are also bonuses." He stated that the biggest bonus is that the site of the Battle of the Little Bighorn is right next door. He can't count the number of out-of-staters coming through who tell him that experiencing this battlefield was on their bucket list. (Approximately 300,000 people per year actually visit the battlefield.) Add to that the big game and bird hunting available in his neighborhood, plus the blue ribbon trout streams that attract fishermen far and wide, and Greg feels that the resulting business environment has provided him and his wife with a foundation for a thriving restaurant.

Towns between Hardin and Ashland:

Crow Agency is noted in the Crow Indian Reservation.

Busby is noted in the Northern Cheyenne Indian Reservation.

Lame Deer is noted in the Northern Cheyenne Indian Reservation.

Crow Indian Proverbs

MAN'S LAW CHANGES WITH HIS UNDER-
STANDING OF MAN. ONLY THE LAWS OF
THE SPIRIT REMAIN ALWAYS THE SAME.

OLD AGE IS NOT AS HONORABLE AS DEATH,
BUT MOST PEOPLE WANT IT.

*"Education is your most powerful weapon.
With education, you are the white man's
equal; without education, you are his victim,
and so shall remain all your lives."*

—by Chief Plenty Coups

Chief Plenty Coups was named a chief of the Crow Tribe at age 28. As a young man and chief, he was a fierce and well-respected warrior. He was thought to have between 50 and 100 feathers on his coup stick, each one representing an act of valor. Many times over, he had fulfilled the four requirements for becoming a chief, which were: touching an enemy without killing him (that is counting coup), taking an enemy's weapon, leading a successful war party, and stealing an enemy's horse.

The **Crow Indian Reservation** was established by treaty in 1868 and is the largest of the seven reservations located in Montana, with three and a half million square miles of land. The Crow tribe has an enrolled membership of about 11,000 people, 7,000 of whom reside on the reservation. Twenty percent speak Crow as their first language.

Towns on the Reservation:

Crow Agency has a population of 1,657 and is the headquarters of the tribe. The re-enactment of the Battle of the Little Bighorn is performed here every year, usually the last weekend in June. This used to be sponsored by the town of Hardin but the Crow Tribe took it over a few years ago.

Battle of the Little Bighorn Cemetery

Fort Smith, population 119, was named for the former Fort C.F. Smith. The Crow name for this town is Annu'ucheepe, "Mouth of canyon." Fort Smith is within three miles of the <u>**Yellowtail Dam**</u> that was created after an agreement was reached between the United States and the Crow Tribe and was named after the famous Crow chairman Robert Yellowtail. The Dam was built over the Bighorn River, with most of the resulting reservoir, which extends for 72 miles, on the Crow Reservation. It was opened in 1967. Bighorn is the name of the river, the mountains, the early town (and ultimately one of the nine original counties) as determined by Lewis and Clark because of their fascination with the sheep that populated the area. Expedition documents state: "Next to the buffalo this was the most sensational animal reported...They walked about and bounded from rock to rock with apparent unconcern where it appeared to me no quadruped could stand firm." The Indians called the area Ah-sah-ta for the great droves of big horn sheep found there. (An interesting fact, at least to me, is that I remember a boat ride down the Bighorn River, before construction of the dam, with my then brother-in-law, Dr. John Smith, at the helm. As we were at the bottom of the canyon, with very, very high rock walls on either side, he pointed out that this view would never be possible after the dam's completion. And, of course, he was right.)

Yellowtail Dam

Lodge Grass, has a population of 456 and is named for Lodge Grass Creek nearby that empties into the Bighorn River. The Indians called the stream Greasy Grass, but because the words greasy and lodge are so similar in the Crow language an interpreter mistakenly used the term Lodge Grass.

Pryor already noted with our stop at Chief Plenty Coups State Park.

St. Xavier already noted prior to tire blowout.

Wyola has a population of 220. It began as a Chicago, Burlington & Quincy Railroad station stop. The Crows called this spot Ammoole, "Where they wait," and the name Wyola somehow came from that term.

The total of all these town populations doesn't come close to the 7,000 indicated as living on the reservation, so I don't know where they all are.

Seal of the Crow Indian Tribe

Because I have no up close and personal experience with the Native American tribes of Montana, I have asked my good friend's daughter, Katie Seibel to comment on her experience working in Crow Agency as a human resources person in the nursing home. "I have lived in Montana most of my life. That being said, I have prejudged the native population most of my life. When I took a job on the Crow Reservation, I had no idea what lay ahead. When I walked through the doors all eyes seemed to be on me with their own prejudices. Their prejudices were based on generations of resentment, unlike mine, based on fear. It took time and lots of learning to erode some of those barriers. I have been blessed more ways than one for my experiences there. I am now a part of a bigger family that I wasn't born in to."

Cheyenne Indian Proverbs

IF A MAN IS AS WISE AS A SERPENT, HE CAN AFFORD TO BE AS HARMLESS AS A DOVE.

DO NOT JUDGE YOUR NEIGHBOR UNTIL YOU WALK TWO MOONS IN HIS MOCCASINS.

"Our land is everything to us...I will tell you one of the things we remember on our land. We remember that our grandfathers paid for it with their lives."
—by John Wooden Legs, Northern Cheyenne

(John Wooden Legs was a Native American author, educator, and the tribal president of the Northern Cheyenne from 1955 to 1968. He was the grandson of Wooden Leg, who fought against General George A. Custer's troops at the Battle of the Little Big Horn in 1876.)

The **Northern Cheyenne Indian Reservation** butts

up against the Crow Indian Reservation to the east. (It's hard to under estimate the wisdom of the United States Government in placing these reservations side by side given the history of bitter animosity between these tribes.) The Cheyenne language belongs to the Algonquian language family. Today, the Cheyenne people are split into two federally recognized nations: the Southern

Cheyenne, who are enrolled in the Cheyenne and Arapaho Tribes in Oklahoma, and the Northern Cheyenne, who are enrolled in the Northern Cheyenne Tribe in Montana. The Northern Cheyenne Indian Reservation was originally called the Tongue River Reservation and was established in 1884 on approximately 690 square miles. It is currently home to about 5,000 Cheyenne people, of the 10,500 who are listed on the enrollment figures.

Towns on the Reservation:

Lame Deer is named after a Miniconjou Lakota chief, who was killed by the U.S. Army in 1877 under a flag of truce south of the town. It was the site of a trading post from the late 1870s. It has a population of 2,086, is the tribal headquarters, and Chief Dull Knife, a two-year College, is located there. And, I would add, that all of us agreed that Lame Deer was the most beautiful spot on our tour. The rolling hills and trees were so green and lush.

Muddy, population 617, was named for the Muddy Creek nearby.

Busby was established in 1904 with Sheridan Busby as the first postmaster. Today's population is 647.

Birney was established in 1886 with Arthur M. Birney as the first postmaster; current population 110.

Ashland, population 957, was originally named Strader, then Birney and now Ashland, possibly because of the abundance of ash trees in the area. Ashland is division headquarters for the Custer National Forest and the home of the **St. Labre Mission and School.** According to St. Labre.org: "The founding of St. Labre Indian School in 1884 was one of the first efforts to care for Native Americans who had been displaced as a result of homesteading. George Yoakam, a former soldier who had been stationed near Miles City, Montana, recognized the hard times experienced by the Northern Cheyenne. He contacted Montana Bishop John Brondel and told him of Indian people who were roaming the Tongue Valley without homes or land – a reservation had not yet been set aside as their land. The bishop purchased land on March 29, 1884, St. Labre Mission and Indian School became a reality. In response to a request by Bishop Brondel for priests and nuns to work among the Northern Cheyenne, three Ursuline nuns and their Superior arrived from Toledo, Ohio. The Mother Superior left after seeing the three to St. Labre and getting them settled. A three-room log cabin served as residence, school, dormitory, and even as a church."

The church is a unique structure, resembling a teepee with a cross projecting out the top, as pictured. The interior is also very unique. Attempted photographs were not at all definitive and words are equally difficult. There are panels, ribbon like panels, strips of stained glass going up three sides, well maybe three places, (because teepees don't have sides) on the teepee, from bottom to top. Spectacular with the light shining through. Quite wonderful to be sure.

St. Labre Mission Church

(According to franciscanmedia.org: Benedict Joseph Labre, after whom the mission is named, "became a pilgrim, traveling from one great shrine to another, living off alms. He wore the rags of a beggar and shared his food with the poor. Filled with the love of God and neighbor, Benedict had special devotion to the Blessed Mother and to the Blessed Sacrament. In Rome, where he lived in the Colosseum for a time, he was called "the poor man of the Forty Hours devotion" and "the beggar of Rome.".…Immediately after his death, in 1783, the people proclaimed him a saint…and he was canonized by Pope Leo XIII in 1881. St. Labre is the patron saint of homeless people.) Since both the reservation and the mission were established in 1884, I can only assume that the Mission preceded the reservation by months.

Seal of the Northern Cheyenne Indian Tribe

Towns between Ashland and Glendive:

Broadus is located in the southeast corner of Montana near the junction of the Powder and Little Powder Rivers. It was named for early settlers, the Broaddus family. The second "d" was mistakenly omitted when the post office was being established in 1900. The Broadus High School is the only high school in Powder River County. County population is 1,607 and the population of Broadus is 518.

Alzada has a population of 23 people. It was originally named Stoneville for Lou Stone who kept a saloon there. Because there was another town in Montana with a similar name, making mail delivery confusing, the name was changed to Alzada n 1885, honoring Mrs. Alzada Sheldon, wife of a pioneer rancher. Today there is a big sign on the main building that reads: Stoneville – Cheap Beer – Lousy Food.

Ekalaka was named after a niece of Sitting Bull, Chief of the Lakota Sioux Indians, named Ijkalaka, meaning "swift one" in the Sioux language. David Harrison Russell was the first homesteader in the area, bringing with him his wife, Ijkalaka. Ekalaka was often nicknamed "puptown" because of the huge numbers of prairie dogs in the area. Current population is 363 people. Surprisingly for a town of that size, it has two banks, one library and three restaurants, at one of which we stopped to eat. In the two minutes we were stopped in front to let off my sister who cannot walk very far, a local woman came by to tell us we couldn't park there. We knew that. Then again, in the less than two minutes we were stopped to let my sister back on, a local law enforcement guy came by to say, "You can't stay here." Again we knew that, but he did not listen, just kept saying, "You can't stay here. You can't stay here." So, I now tell people we were kicked out of Ekalaka by two very alert citizens of the 363 who live there.

Baker was first called Lorraine, but later changed to honor A. G. Baker, a construction engineer for the Milwaukee Railroad, when the post office was established in 1908. To my surprise, when passing through, we noticed that Baker was built around a small lake. It is fed by a natural spring and was developed by the Milwaukee Railroad to feed their steam engines. When I talked with my cousin's wife, Shirley Cadby, who grew up in Baker (1936 to 1954), she said the lake was the place you would find all the children in town during the warm months. Shirley's parents owned The Green Dragon Bar and Restaurant on Main Street and they lived above the bar. In a town of roughly 3,000 people then, there were at least five other bars. Shirley says: "I loved my life there. It wasn't perfect, but everybody on Main Street took care of me and I loved it." Current population of Baker is 1,756.

Wibaux (pronounced "WEE bow") was first called Keith and then Mungusville, before being named after Pierre Wibaux, a Huguenot who settled in the area and became the largest cattleman in the state. At his peak he had 75,000 head of cattle. (Huguenots are French Protestants who follow the teachings of John Calvin, dating back to the 16th century.) Current Wibaux population is 600. Wibaux is seven miles from Beach, North Dakota.

Glendive is 287 miles from my cabin on the Stillwater River that is considered to be in Nye, Montana.

Glendive was named for Glendive Creek which was itself considered to be a corruption of Glendale the name given to it by Sir St.George Gore, a wealthy Irish nobleman and avid sportsman noted for the following expedition. Sir Gore hired Jim Bridger to be his guide to hunt the Powder River region. His entourage included: a few companions, 40 servants, 112 horses, 12 yoke of oxen, 14 hunting dogs, an arsenal of arms and ammunition, 6 wagons and 21 carts loaded with every luxury known at the time. They slaughtered so much game that the Indians were resentful. Glendive population is 5,126. The dinosaur museum in Glendive is presented from the perspective that human beings did not evolve from apes but were created as human beings. It was founded by Otis Kline and is now owned by the non-profit organization Advancing Creation Truth. The museum promotes digs in the area for continued search of dinosaur remains and fossils.

Medicine Rocks State Park is located about 25 miles west-southwest of Baker and 11 miles north of Ekalaka. Per Wikipedia: "The park is named for the 'Medicine Rocks,' a series of sandstone pillars similar to hoodoos some 60 to 80 feet high with eerie undulations, holes, and tunnels in them. The rocks contain numerous examples of Native American rock art and are considered a sacred place by Plains Indians. As a young rancher, future president Theodore Roosevelt said Medicine Rocks was 'as fantastically beautiful a place as I have ever seen.' The park is 330 acres in size, sits at 3,379 feet in elevation, and is managed by the Montana Department of Fish, Wildlife and Parks. It was listed on the National Register of Historic Places in 2017 and designated as a certified International Dark Sky Sanctuary in 2020."

Medicine Rocks State Park

Makoshika State Park "('ma-KO-sh(ih)kuh' from the Lakota *Maco sica,* meaning 'bad land' or 'land of bad spirits' is a nature preserve and public recreation area located on the southeast side of Glendive. The state park encompasses badlands containing dinosaur fossils and rock from the Hell Creek Formation. It is the largest of Montana's state parks at more than 11,000 acres," per Wikipedia. We parked our motor home there for the evening. ("The **Hell Creek Formation** is an intensively studied division of mostly Upper Cretaceous and some lower Paleocene rocks in North America, named for exposures studied along **Hell Creek**, near Jordan, Montana. The formation stretches over portions of Montana, North Dakota, South Dakota, and Wyoming. In Montana, the Hell Creek Formation overlies the Fox Hills Formation. The site of Pompeys Pillar National Monument is a small isolated section of the Hell Creek Formation. In 1966, the Hell Creek Fossil Area was designated as a National Natural Landmark by the National Park Service.")

Makoshika State Park

Sidney is about 338 miles from my cabin on the Stillwater River that is considered to be in Nye, Montana.

Sidney was originally called Eureka, but because of a duplication of names in the state (evidently not an uncommon occurrence), it was named after Sidney Walters, a young man whose parents were pioneers in the area. At the time Sidney's parents were staying with Hiram Otis who was the Justice of the Peace. It was he who decided that Sidney was a good name for a town. Population is 6,416. My first cousin (our fathers were brothers) Susan Zimmerman and her husband Bill, met us for lunch at The Brewery. Again, good food and good company. When I asked Sue if she would comment on living in Sidney, this was her response: "Sidney has been an interesting place to live. When we first moved here to teach school in 1969, people would stare at us trying to figure out who we were and what we were doing in their town. Two oil booms have come and, at least mostly, gone in the ensuing years. It is now great to see someone you DO know when out and about. Even though we are a long way from most of the state, the friendliness and helpfulness of people in this corner of the state makes the distance to the bigger, and supposedly better, places totally worth it."

<u>Towns between Sidney and Scobey:</u>

Culbertson has a population of 665 people. It was named for Alexander Culbertson, a fur trapper and mountain man.

As county boundaries shifted over the years, Culbertson has been in five different counties: Bighorn, Dawson, Custer, Valley and presently Roosevelt. At one time Culbertson had 13 saloons open for business 24 hours a day.

Froid was suggested as a name for the town by division engineer Charles Walker, who took it from an old Nebraska map. The name means "cold" in French and that seemed appropriate for a town close to both North Dakota and Canada. Current population is 384.

Medicine Lake was originally named Flandrem by Edward Stubban for his home town in Norway. The town moved about 2 miles with the construction of the Great Northern Railway in 1910. The name was changed to Medicine Lake after the nearby lake which the Assiniboine Indians referred to as Bda wauka, meaning "Medicine water." Town population is 183.

Antelope, population 47, is named for a nearby creek. Large herds of antelope would water at the stream. It once had a bigger population but over the years better roads to the south siphoned off business, and the "Biggest Little City in Eastern Montana" sank into decline. The U. S. Navy has a gunboat named "Antelope."

Plentywood has a population of 1,527. It is named for a nearby creek. The story behind the naming of the creek involves a search for firewood and being directed to a place where "plenty of wood" could be found.

Redstone has 31 residents. The name was suggested by the wife of Olaf Bergh who noticed all the red shale in the area.

Flaxville got its name from the fact that flax was the only grain grown in the area in the early days. The original settlement was named Boyer and was located about two and a half miles southwest of the present town. It was moved to its present location when the Great Northern Railroad came through. Population 23.

Madoc has no population registered as living there. Homesteaders arrived in Madoc in 1909. In 1910, a post office was established under the name of Orville. The Great Northern Railway arrived in 1913. The name was changed to Madoc in 1915. The train doesn't roll by on these tracks anymore and the post office closed in 1963. Although Madoc is now considered a Montana Ghost Town, the green sign identifying the location of a town remains on the highway.

Scobey is about 406 miles from my cabin on the Stillwater River that is considered to be in Nye, Montana.

Scobey was named by local rancher Mansfield Daniels, after whom Daniels County is named, for his friend Major Charles Richardson Anderson Scobey, a cattleman from the Glendive area who served as a Montana Territory legislator and an Indian agent at Fort Peck and Poplar. The two main employers in Scobey are Nemont Telephone Company (which is the telephone service I have at my cabin on the Stillwater) and the U. S. Border Patrol, as Scobey is only 14.5 miles from the Scobey-Coronach Canadian border crossing. Population in the 2020 census was 999. Located on 20 acres just west of Scobey is Pioneer Town. Thirty-five historic buildings have been restored to depict a town in the early 1900's. The Rex Theatre, in my opinion, the most impressive of all the buildings, is home to the Dirty Shame Show which we were unable to see as that only happens during Pioneer Days, the last weekend in June. The theater was in operation until 1941 and was moved to Pioneer Town in 1971. Other buildings include: family homes, doctor's office, blacksmith shop, dentist's office, three churches (Episcopal, Eastern Orthodox, Catholic), women's clothing store, bank, school, saloon, general store and outdoor jail that looked like a big metal cage in which you might keep dogs, temporarily. There was no protection from the weather and no privacy of any kind. Pioneer Town is definitely worth seeing.

Pioneer Town in Scobey, Montana

Towns between Scobey and Fort Peck:

Wolf Point is noted with towns on the Fort Peck Indian Reservation.

Frazer is noted with towns on the Fort Peck Indian Reservation.

Nashua is situated where Porcupine Creek runs into the Milk River. The waters of these two streams flow into the Missouri near the Fort Peck Dam. Nashua is thought to be an Indian word meaning "meeting of two streams." Nashua boomed only while the Fort Peck Dam was being built. Current population is 326.

Park Grove appears not to be a town in Montana, even though there is a green sign on the highway saying it is.

Fort Peck is about 373 miles from my cabin on the Stillwater River that is considered to be in Nye, Montana.

The name **Fort Peck** came from Col. Campbell K. Peck who, with his partner Elias H. Durfee, had the trading firm of Durfee and Peck. In 1867, company employee Abe Farwell constructed the Fort Peck trading post along the Missouri River where trading with the Sioux and Assiniboine Indians was primary. From a trading post it became an Indian agency from 1873 to 1878, and eventually in 1934 a new town to house Army Corps of Engineers employees involved in construction of the <u>Fort Peck Dam</u>. There were over 10,000 employees at the peak, plus the additional people who had come to provide needed services. (My father, uncle and grandfather were three of those people. My mom, dad, and two sisters lived there temporarily while my father worked as an automobile mechanic. My uncle and grandfather were carpenters who were busy building needed structures. As a matter of fact, you can go on line to YouTube, PBS, Public Broadcasting System, and watch the documentary entitled "Fort Peck Dam," which I recommend highly. At the 35 minute marker there is a picture of two little girls with a birthday cake and a woman standing in the background. Those two little girls are my sisters, Dione and Glenda, and the cake is for Dione's fourth birthday. The woman standing in the background is my Aunt Altha Dahl, my father's sister.) The current population of the town of Fort

Peck, according to the 2020 census, is 239 people. The Fort Peck Dam was a major project of the New Deal under President Franklin Roosevelt, started in 1933 and finished in 1940. It is located on the Missouri River in northeastern Montana. Fort Peck Lake, created as a result of the dam's completion, is 130 miles long, 200 feet deep and has a shoreline of 1,520 miles, making it the fifth largest artificial lake in the U.S. They were not offering tours of the dam when we were there and from the road it looked like a long rolling hill. Nothing like this picture.

Fort Peck Dam
(largest hydraulically filled earth dam in the world)

The town of Fort Peck was very impressive. It has big beautiful trees and a very hospitable residential area. It is obvious that some of the structures, both private homes and office buildings, are originals from the dam building days. For sure, the theater was built in the 1930's by the Army Corps of Engineers to provide around the clock entertainment for the dam workers. The theatre is now a Historic Landmark and is now owned by the Fort Peck Fine Arts Council and has live performances on weekends in the summer. The two that we saw were: History of America (Abridged) and Forever Plaid. History of America is a comedy about which I wasn't very pleased, but I will offer that I was the problem not the play. They talked so fast and the sound system messed with my ears, so I missed most of what was said. I think there were many very clever lines, but they went right past me. Forever Plaid was awesome. The quartet of four young men sang songs from the 1950's that I absolutely loved. The singing itself was not superb, but it was very good with occasional harmonies that were exceptional. I would see hat again in a heartbeat.

Fort Peck Theater

Fort Peck has an Interpretive Center that gives a thorough history of the dam and general information about the current local fish and game and that of the ancient past, dinosaurs. It, too, is well done and worth seeing.

And then, there is the dam itself and the lake that backs up behind it. The dam looks like a long, big mound of earth. The lake is very large and an attraction to boaters and water skiers, including our group. But, let me tell you what we had to do to get to the Rock Creek Marina. We drove something like 30 miles from Fort Peck on State Highway 24, then a right turn on Rock Creek North (there is also a Rock Creek South and a Rock Creek West so be careful) which is a gravel road, and finally, five miles on a dirt road with no signage warning of conditions. Those conditions were: single lane, more of a path than a road, and no obvious maintenance. Remember we are driving a motor home, a rather large motor home. We saw no water, no boats or campers, no people until we were right on top of it. And then, there were campers and people everywhere, including what appeared to be permanently placed manufactured/modular homes and lots of boats. The boats were launched into a small bay which led to the large lake. The shoreline had no trees and no buildings. It was an overcast day and the water was too cold for comfortable swimming, but still most enjoyable. Holli and Frank had rented a pontoon boat so we two old ladies could actually get on board. Another worthwhile experience. As we were leaving, after getting off that miserable dirt road, we saw the following sign that should also have been posted on the Rock Creek North dirt portion of the road.

Assiniboine Indian Proverb
BE BRAVE, WHERE BRAVERY IS HONORABLE.

Sioux Indian Proverb
WITH ALL THINGS AND IN ALL THINGS, WE ARE RELATIVES.

"Why should Indian people be forced to live under a law made some 80 years ago? That is the year in which the Indian Commissioner referred to Indians as 'wild beasts!'"
—by Dolly Smith Cusker Akers

(**Dolly Akers or Dolly Smith Cusker Akers** was the first woman elected to the Tribal Executive Board of the Assiniboine and Sioux Tribes on the Fort Peck Indian Reservation and the first Native American elected to the Montana Legislature in 1932.)

The **Fort Peck Indian Reservation**, which is home to the Assiniboine, also known as Nakoda, and the Sioux (pronounced Sue), also known as Dakota, lies 50 miles south of the Canadian border, 40 miles west of the North Dakota border, with the Missouri River defining its southern perimeter. The 1,456 square miles of land were designated as a reservation by Presidential order of Ulysses Grant in 1871. The Assiniboine are relatives of the Dakota tribes, and they speak a similar language;

however, they have always been politically distinct from the Sioux. In fact, they were often at war with each other. (Here we go again, only this time they share the same reservation. Interesting philosophy on someone's part within the United States government.) There are an estimated 11,786 enrolled tribal members, of whom approximately 6,000 reside on or near the reservation.

Towns on the Reservation:

Brockton, population 319, was established in 1904 but not incorporated until 1952.

Frazer was established by the St. Paul, Minneapolis and Manitoba Railway in 1888. It was named for the foreman of a grading crew when the railroad was being built. Current population is 344.

Lustre is an unincorporated community of about 200. It was founded in the early 1900s, primarily by Mennonite families who homesteaded the area located on the Fort Peck Indian Reservation. The community of modern-day Lustre consists of two churches and two schools. Working together, both churches support an active AWANA ministry as well as Beacon Bible Camp ministry. (AWANA is a world-wide non-profit ministry focused on providing Bible-based evangelism and discipleship solutions for ages 2-18.) The name Lustre was selected for its euphonic sound.

Poplar is the headquarters for the tribes on the Fort Peck Reservation. It is located at the confluence of the Poplar and Missouri Rivers and was named Poplar because of the abundance of poplar trees in the area, which was shortened from the original Poplar Creek Agency. Current population is 852, and Poplar is the home of the main campus of the Fort Peck Community College.

Reserve was platted in 1911 as Wakea, but that name was changed to Reserve in 1912 when the post office was established. The assumption is that Reserve is simply a shortened version of reservation. Current population is 35.

Wolf Point, with a population of 2,739, is by far the largest town on the Fort Peck Reservation. Wolf Point's Wild Horse Stampede, held every year in the second week of July, is the oldest rodeo in Montana, and has been called the "Grandaddy of Montana Rodeos." The most generally accepted version of how Wolf Point got it's name follows: One winter a party of wolfers, who made up the lowest rung of the social ladder in frontier life, captured several hundred grey wolves in very cold weather. They hauled the carcasses into camp and stacked the frozen bodies facing the river where the steamboats came in. The grisly pile of wolves gave the town its name.

Fort Kipp was named for Captain James Kipp, who commanded the fort for many years. He was a fur trader, respected by the Indians and married to an Indian woman. The current Fort Kipp has about 360 people.

Oswego was established somewhere in the 1890s. It was named after Oswego, New York, as many of the early settlers came from there. In 1972, one of the worst prairie fires decimated Oswego forcing its 75 residents to reconsider living there. Current population is about 40.

Seal of the Assiniboine and Sioux Tribes
on the Fort Peck Reservation

Towns between Fort Peck and Sleeping Buffalo Resort:

Glasgow is located on the Milk River just 17 miles from Fort Peck. At a population of 3,332, it is the most populous city for over 110 miles, thus making it an important economic hub for a large region in Eastern Montana. Both Amtrak and the National Weather Service operate facilities in Glasgow that link the city to the surrounding region. It was named after Glasgow, Scotland.

Hinsdale was named after a town in New Hampshire, after a spin of the globe, according to one version and according to another, a town in Illinois. At its peak Hinsdale had 1,200 people, currently 284.

Saco got its name in that same globe spinning manner for a town in Maine. I guess the Great Northern Railway had so many towns to name that was the most efficient method. Other versions of where Saco got its name is that it is a diminutive of Sacajawea or from Sack-ow, an Indian tribe in Maine. Current population is 279. The Sleeping Buffalo Rocks nearby, when viewed from a distance, resemble buffalo lying down. Legend has it that an Indian hunting party advanced on the herd of sleeping buffalo only to find that they had turned to stone. The largest rock was covered with picture writings. Young Indians pinched pieces of flesh from their bodies to leave on the stone to get "good medicine" for the hunt. The warm water for the Sleeping Buffalo Hot Springs Resort comes from those hills. The swimming pool is large and quite nice. Worth a stop.

Assiniboine Indian Proverb

MOST OF US DO NOT LOOK AS HANDSOME TO
OTHERS AS WE DO TO OURSELVES.

Indian Tribe Unknown Proverb

TELL ME AND I'LL FORGET.
SHOW ME, AND I MAY NOT REMEMBER.
INVOLVE ME, AND I'LL UNDERSTAND.

The **Fort Belknap Indian Reservation** is located 40 miles south of the Canadian border and 20 miles north of the Missouri River. This reservation was established by an act of congress in 1888 and has a population of 3,429 people which is very close to the estimated total enrollment figure of 4000. It is comprised of approximately one thousand square miles and is home to the Assiniboine (Nakoda) and Gros Ventre (pronounced Grow Vont) (Aaniiih) tribes. According to Wikipedia: Nakoda means Generous Ones, but they were called "one who cooks with stones" by the Chippewa. "The Nakoda would heat rocks and put them in rawhide pots to heat water and cook food. The Nakoda peoples live on both the Fort Belknap and Fort Peck Indian Reservations in Montana and on several reserves in Saskatchewan and Alberta, Canada, where they are generally known as Stoney. The origin of the name Aaniiih, (meaning the White Clay People) is unclear. Many believe that they painted themselves with white clay found along the Saskatchewan River for ceremony, like the northern Arapaho. Early French fur trappers and traders named this tribe Gros Ventre. Other tribes in the area referred to them as the "Water Falls People". Lacking a common language, they used physical signs to indicate some terms. The sign for waterfall was the passing of the hands over the stomach. The French traders interpreted this as meaning "big belly" and called the Aaniiih the Gros Ventre, meaning "big belly" in the French language."

Towns on the Reservation:

Fort Belknap Agency is located at the junction of U.S. Route 2 and Montana Highway 66 and is the headquarters for the tribes. It is home to the Aaniiih Nakoda College and has 1,542 residents.

Hays was named for Major Hays who helped the Gros Ventre tribe get established in this reservation. The Bureau of Catholic Indian Missions built St. Paul's Mission Church at Hays in 1887. Current population is 930.

Lodge Pole has a population of 308.

Seal of the Fort Belknap Reservation

Towns between Sleeping Buffalo Resort and Roberts:

Malta was another of those town named by a spin of the globe, for the Mediterranean Island by the same name. It was the Saturday night haven for cowpokes from the Canadian border to the Missouri. One of the best preserved dinosaurs ever discovered and one of only four that were fossilized is a 77-million-year-old *Brachylophosaurus* nicknamed Leonardo, unearthed north of Malta in 2000. Current population 2,028.

Grass Range is another of those "wide spots in the road" so I'm surprised that it has a population of 121. The name came from the fact that it was located in the middle of the finest grass land the cattlemen had ever seen. Oh, and just so you know, it was 112 miles on Highway 191 South before we came to the first town – Grass Range.

Roundup served as a place for cattlemen to "round up" their cattle along the Musselshell River. It was the trailhead in the Great Montana Centennial Cattle Drive in 1989, and now drives happen annually. Population is 1,723.

Billings (my home town) is covered in the "My Neighborhood" section.

Laurel is noted in the "My Neighborhood" section.

Rockvale, Joliet and Boyd were all noted in the beginning of the "Eastern Montana" section.

It is very important for me to comment on the general take away from this trip. I have always thought of eastern Montana as being dull, dreary, dusty, drab, in short boring, long expanses of nothingness. None of that applies to this experience. Everything was green, green, green. Even the "long expanses of nothingness" were green and therefore beautiful. Everything was lush and green and wonderful.

When we arrived back home on June 13, 2022, we came face to face with the results of the highest water levels in the Stillwater River, Rock Creek and the Yellowstone River in recorded history. Remember this is MY Stillwater River. It is the Stillwater River that flows within 20 feet of my cabin (that is considered to be in Nye, Montana). Rock Creek flows by my companions' home in Roberts. The Yellowstone River flows between me and my daughter's home in Columbus.

First, Holli and Frank discovered that a cabin on their property, in which their youngest son lived, that was on the banks of Rock Creek, was gone. Completely gone, along with all his belongings. In addition, they lost about one half acre of property. No one hurt – they were all on the road with me or somewhere else, so much for which to be grateful.

I was immediately informed that there most likely was no damage to my cabin but I was not going to be able to get home – two bridges gone. My decision was to go to my daughter's home on the other side of the Yellowstone River, so I needed to do that right away in anticipation of that bridge being closed.

Two days later I was able to get back across the Yellowstone Bridge and to my cabin by following a circuitous route: over a bridge they were able to save across Rosebud Creek in Absarokee; follow state road 420 to the end of the pavement; turn left onto Grove Creek Road, a dirt road; travel for about 6.5 miles until get to state road 419; turn right and travel up to Carter's Camp (about 17 miles); turn right and cross the West Fork Bridge; then proceed down Stillwater Road, a gravel road, for about ten miles; get to Midnight Canyon Bridge and MY CABIN. Ordinarily this trip would be 12 miles, total. Within all that there is much for which to be grateful: nobody hurt, no damage to cabin, dogs well cared for and very happy to be home.

As was obvious by the national news, there was a considerable amount of damage in other areas. All northern entrances to our precious Yellowstone Park closed indefinitely because of massive road damage. Red Lodge, Montana, had Rock Creek flowing down their main street, so one can only imagine the damage that caused. Lost homes and property and undoubtedly damage that we will never hear about. Again, there is also much for which to be grateful.

"Everything is so big—the sky, the mountains, the wind-swept flatlands—it sinks into you, it shapes your body and your dreams."

- Christopher Paolini, author

WESTERN MONTANA TOUR

Days One and Two:
Travel from Columbus to Ronan (358 Miles) Through Reed Point, Greycliff, Big Timber, Springdale, Livingston, Bozeman, Belgrade, Manhattan, Logan, Three Forks, Butte, Deer Lodge, Garrison, Clinton, Bonner, Missoula, Arlee and St. Ignatius

    Interests: Arlee, 1,000 Buddhas (Jocko Valley)

                 St. Ignatius Mission

                 Flathead Lake Activities

Camp at Private Home in Ronan both Days

Day Three:
Travel from Ronan to Libby (191 Miles) Through Charlo, Moiese, Dixon, Paradise, Plains, Thompson Falls, Noxon, Heron and Troy

    Interests: Dixon to Heron <u>most</u> scenic route in Montana

                 Libby Dam

                 Koocanusa Reservoir and Bridge

Camp at Libby Creek Campground

Days Four and Five:
Travel from Libby to Glacier Park (121 Miles) Through Marion, Kila, Kalispell, Columbia Falls and Hungry Horse

    Interests: Conrad Mansion

                 Bus Tour of Park

Camp in Hungry Horse both Days

Day Six:
    Travel from Glacier Park to Cut Bank (170 Miles) Through Hungry Horse, Coram, West Glacier, St. Mary's and Browning
        Interests: Jarvenpaa Ranch
                      Blackfeet Museum
                      St. Mary's Lake
    Camp at Jarvenpaa Ranch

Day Seven:
    Travel from Cut Bank to Great Falls (120 Miles) Through Valier and Brady
        Interests: Five Waterfalls
                      Giant Springs State Park
                      C.M. Russell Museum
                      Buffalo Jump State Park
                      Sleeping Giant
                Lewis & Clark Interpretive Center
    Camp at Great Falls KOA Holiday

Day Eight:
    Travel from Great Falls to Helena (91 Miles) Through Ulm, Cascade, Craig and Wolf Creek
        Interests: State Capitol
                      Old Governor's Mansion
                      Cathedral
    Camp at Helena Campground and RV Park

Day Nine:
    Travel from Helena to Butte (68 Miles) Through Montana City, Clancy, Jefferson City, Boulder and Basin
        Interests: Serbian Church
                      Our Lady of the Rockies (The only way to get there is on a bus tour)
    Camp at Butte KOA Journey

Day Ten:
    Travel from Butte back to Columbus (186 Miles)

Columbus is about 26 miles (under normal conditions when all the bridges are functional) from my cabin on the Stillwater River considered to be in Nye, Montana.

Columbus is the only incorporated town in Stillwater County and is the county seat. This community originated as a stagecoach station on the Yellowstone River and became a major stop for the Northern Pacific Railroad. It seemed that the name was changed on a whim going through such names as Eagle's Nest, Sheep Dip and Stillwater, before being changed to Columbus in 1893. Historians are not sure if it was named to honor Christopher Columbus or the town of Columbus, Minnesota. Its claim to fame came when stone from the Columbus quarry was chosen for construction of the Montana State Capital building in Helena. This provided many years of economic security for the town. Current population is 1,857. (Columbus is also included in the My Neighborhood section.)

<u>Towns between Columbus and Ronan:</u>

Reed Point was originally registered as Reed only, in honor of Harry Reed who ran a stage station. That was changed to Reed Point in 1906. The center of town was a large store with big windows and a very large sign: A. L. Guthrie General Merchandise. Current population is 247.

Big Timber was named by William Clark for the large cottonwood trees that lined the local creek (also called Big Timber Creek). Population 1,736. The view of the Crazy Mountains is spectacular from Big Timber.

Springdale is one of those wide spots in the road, just off of I-90, between Big Timber and Livingston. It was named for the many springs that originate in the area including Hunter Hot Springs. It was here that the Indians stole all of William Clark's horses in 1806, so he had to travel down the Yellowstone in bull boats. Population in 2020 census was 19 people (which would make it tied with Ismay for smallest in Montana). The only reason for its inclusion here is that I spent some time there as a child. My mother's sister, Edith Cadby, and her family, my uncle and cousins, lived there; my uncle owned and operated the local mercantile store. My memories of those occasions include a huge barrel filled with pickles in the store, getting to go through the store and get whatever I wanted (the proverbial kid in a candy store), riding a horse from which I got bucked off and putting pennies on the railroad track so the passing train would smash them flatter than they started out.

Livingston has a population of 7,696 people. It began in 1882 when railroad surveyors camped on the site and called it Clark City in honor of William Clark who arrived at this point in 1806. The first settlement was called Benson's Landing and was later changed to Livingston for Crawford Livingston, a director of the Northern Pacific Railroad, upon which the town has depended throughout its development.

Bozeman is almost completely surrounded by the Rocky Mountains. It was originally called Missouri because it was populated with immigrants from Missouri. However, it was later named after John Bozeman who blazed a trail across Wyoming and guided many immigrants into the valley. He and Jim Bridger were friendly rivals, both of them guiding immigrants. John Bozeman was killed by the Piegan Indians while traversing a very narrow part of the valley. As was noted earlier, Bozeman is the home of Montana State University, a land grant university established in 1893. It is highly respected for many programs, perhaps the most popular of which is the engineering school. Student population last year was 16,703. Current city population is 53,293, but the surrounding area within Gallatin County is growing rapidly with a county total of almost 119,000 people (as already mentioned in Montana History). In recent years Bozeman has become a sought after place to live, making real estate values soar: Median Price of a Single Family Home - $837,500, Median Price of a Townhome - $525,000, Median Price of a Condo - $505,000.

Dick Ford, who is married to my former husband's sister, was born, grew up and graduated from high school in Bozeman. He then proceeded to graduate from the University of Montana at Missoula, but has always considered Bozeman his home. His comments follow: "I live in California, but I am a Montanan. How can I claim that after living almost 60 years in California? Because in my heart I always will have the desire to return to the mountains, the lakes, the small towns, the blue skies, and the wide open spaces; a place where one can get away and enjoy fresh air and be alone; a place many dream of but will not understand why. It is an itch I cannot scratch, no matter how I try. Montana pride is in my heart and deep in my soul."

Belgrade was named by a Serbian from Belgrade, now Yugoslavia. He was a special guest on the train taking the president of the railroad to Gold Creek for the ceremony of driving the last spike, denoting the completion of the Northern Pacific Railroad. Belgrade is only 10 miles from Bozeman and is the home of the (maybe not so appropriately named) Bozeman Airport. It is also subject to the same population boom numbering 9,184 according to the 2020 census, and 11,075 today in 2022. Compare that to the 1,057 in 1960 when my aunt, uncle and cousins lived there. My uncle once again owned a grocery store and the family lived in the basement underneath with a kitchen and bathroom in the back of the store. The store burned to the ground in 1959, the family losing everything. According to my now deceased aunt Edith, the most difficult of all the losses was family pictures. There was no way to replace them. All lost.

Manhattan has a population of 1,950, also experiencing the population boom because of its proximity to Bozeman (20 miles northwest). It was named by a group of New York investors who had purchased a lot of land in the area. Previous names were Moreland and Hamilton. Its location was determined by the Northern Pacific Railroad.

Logan was another railroad town that acquired their right-of-way from Adelia Logan in 1885. One more possibility for the name is in honor of Captain William Logan, who came to Montana in 1872, taking part in General Baker's campaign against the Indians in 1872 to 1876. I guess you can take your pick. It was Originally called Cannon House but changed to Logan in 1889. Current population 17. (Looks like there is yet another even smaller than Ismay. Oops.)

"Sacagawea recognizes the country and assures us that... the three forks are at no great distance. This piece of information has cheered the spirits of the party."

—William Clark

Three Forks is located a few miles from the intersection of Interstate 90 and U.S. Route 287 in southwestern Montana, between Butte (56 miles to the west) and Bozeman (32 miles to the east). Three Forks was founded in September of 1908 by John Q. Adams, a land agent for the Milwaukee Railroad. The town's name was a natural because of it's location at the confluence of three rivers: the Jefferson (named for President Thomas Jefferson), the Madison (named for Secretary of State James Madison), and the Gallatin (named for Secretary of the Treasury Albert Gallatin). These three rivers join to form the Missouri River which is the longest river in North America. (The Missouri dumps into the Mississippi, which journeys on to the Gulf of Mexico.) These three rivers were named by Meriwether Lewis in 1805 when he and William Clark visited the area. Obviously, this means that Three Forks was a stop on the Lewis and Clark Trail extending from Pittsburgh, Pennsylvania, to the mouth of the Columbia River in Oregon.

Statue of Sacagawea in front of Sacajawea Hotel in Three Forks

"Amazing the things you find when you bother to search for them."

—Sacagawea.

Another famous name from this era and adventure is "Sacaja-wea," whose name is also written as Sacagawea, the Indian woman best known as the interpreter and guide for Lewis and Clark. She was captured by the Minataree tribe (called by the Canadians Gros Ventres of the Missouri, but by themselves Hidatsa, originally part of the Crow nation) near Three Forks and later returned to the area with Lewis and Clark. The city of Three Forks honors her with a statue in a park on their main street, directly across from the Sacajawea Inn/Hotel that was built in 1910 and is listed on the National Register of Historic Places.

According to the 2020 census, Three Forks is home to 1,989 people, two of whom are my first cousin, more like a sister, Robin Gay Cadby and her husband, Rodney (Toby) Sorensen. They were high school classmates and both graduated from Three Forks High in 1958. Toby was born in Idaho but shortly was moved to Montana and has lived here ever since, in Three Forks since the age of 12. After studying at both Montana State College in Bozeman and Montana School of Mines (renamed Montana Technological University/Montana Tech) in Butte, he graduated from MSC, now MSU, and followed in his father's footsteps to become a beekeeper, later buying his father's business. He married, had two children, divorced and later married Robin. Robin had lived in several different towns in Montana, Los Angeles in California, and a couple in Oregon before her father purchased a grocery store in Belgrade and her mother got a teaching job in Three Forks. That meant that Robin went from the 8th to the 12th grades in Three Forks, and of course, Toby was in her classes. However, she too married someone else, had two daughters, moved around the United States; Oregon, New Mexico, Tennessee, Mississippi, and Oklahoma, and traveled to the countries of Canada, Mexico, Guatamala, El Salvador, Honduras, Argentina, England and Jamaica, divorced and did not return to Montana until she and Toby got married 30 years ago. Toby is a member of the Three Forks Masonic Lodge and has been Worshipful Master (In ancient times, the word "Worshipful" meant "Respected," and the position is equivalent to being president, a respected position) twice and became Potentate (again like being president) of the Algeria Shrine. (I attended his installation and have since then taken great delight in addressing him as the "Illustrious Sir" which is how he was addressed following the ceremony and Robin as "First Lady.") In addition to Toby's high position in the Shrine, now as a Past Potentate, Robin was Curator of the Headwaters Heritage Museum for 20 years and is currently on the Three Forks Area Historical Society Board of Directors, so they are both major contributors to the Montana culture.

Toby says: "Montana has changed. I liked Montana best when it was possible to be free to roam, to go where you wanted to go to fish, etc. We used to only have to be sure to open and close the gates! All that has changed now with leasing of land by fishing guides and property ownership. Now all gates are locked. I like Montana's climate and the lower population than other states, but I feel that the population in the Gallatin Valley area is growing too fast, especially in the Bozeman-Belgrade-Four Corners area." And Robin adds: "Having lived in a variety of places with different climates and scenery, I feel Montana rates at the top because of the clean air, beautiful scenery and friendliness of the people. Most folks here have a friendly 'hello' and a smile or a wave. Seems like that is how you can tell the 'home grown' from the newcomers. But, Montana has always meant 'home' to me, no matter where I was living." Amen. I think I've said those very words.

Just a brief explanation of the Masons and Shriners: Masonry is a fraternal organization that dates back to the early 18th century and before. The Grand Lodge of Pennsylvania claims to be the first in the United States having been established in 1731. George Washington, Benjamin Franklin, Paul Revere and John Hancock were some of the founding fathers who were Masons. The Masons are a "social and philanthropic organization meant to make its members lead more virtuous and socially oriented lives," says Margaret Jacob, professor of history at University of California,

Los Angeles, and author of *Living the Enlightenment: Freemasonry and Politics in Eighteenth-Century Europe*. In order to be a Shriner, a man must first be a Mason, at least 21 years of age, be of good moral character and have a personal belief in a Supreme Being (the definition of a Supreme Being is up to you.) Shriners were formerly known as the "Ancient Arabic Order of the Nobles of the Mystic Shrine." This Masonic society was established in 1870 and describe themselves as: a fraternity based on fun, fellowship, and the Masonic principles of brotherly love, belief, and truth. With the emphasis on fun and fellowship they adopted the Arabic theme using an elaborately staged musical comedy.as the guide for their principle activities, hence their officers are named: Potentate, Rabban, High Priest and Prophet, and Oriental Guide. So, long story short, a Mason isn't necessarily a Shriner, but a Shriner must be a Mason.

Butte is noted on the route home.

Deer Lodge had many names before it became Deer Lodge officially. It was in the valley that was called "Lodge of the White-Tailed Deer" by the Indians. The French trappers called it "La Loge Chevreuils." There was a natural salt lick in the valley that brought the deer there in droves. It was called Cottonwood by the gold miners because of the abundance of Cottonwood trees along the Clark Fork River that bisects the town. It was called LaBarge City in honor of Captain LaBarge who arrived in 1802 to start a trading post. Citizens formed the Deer Lodge Town Company and Deer Lodge City, then just plain Deer Lodge in 1896. Deer Lodge is home to the Montana Territorial Penitentiary built in 1871 with convict labor, before Montana became a state in 1889. That prison remained in use, with many additions and alterations, until 1979 when a new facility was built five miles outside of Deer Lodge. The original penitentiary now houses five different museums: Montana Auto Museum, Yesterday's Playthings, Frontier Montana, Powell County Museum, and Old Montana Prison. Current population of Deer Lodge is 2,893.

Garrison is named for William Lloyd Garrison, an anti-slavery leader. The belief is that a Yankee Civil War veteran came to the area and named it after the man he most admired. Population 88.

Clinton is an old mining and lumber town, originally known as Betters' Station, named for Austin Betters, a homesteader. The Northern Pacific Railroad men called it Wallace, but the postal department would not accept that name. It was also called Pine Grove, which was very descriptive, and Blossberg, but ended up with Clinton, after General Sir Henry Clinton. Population is 661.

Bonner has a population of 1,404 people. It was named for E. L. Bonner, an early Missoula settler and first president of the Missoula and Bitterroot Valley Railroad. Bonner was home to one of the state's first large sawmills. (Bonner's Ferry in Idaho is also named for this Montana lumber magnate.

"The world is full of bastards, the number increasing rapidly the further one gets from Missoula, Montana."
—Norman Maclean, A River Runs Through It

Missoula is located along the Clark Fork River near its confluence with the Bitterroot and Blackfoot Rivers in western Montana and at the convergence of five mountain ranges. Missoula was founded in 1860 as Hellgate Trading Post while still part of Washington Territory. By 1866, the settlement had moved east, 5 miles upstream, and had been renamed Missoula Mills, later shortened to Missoula. The name "Missoula" came from the Salish name for the Clark Fork River, *nmesuletkw*, which roughly translates as "place of frozen water." The Montana Legislature chose Missoula as the site for the state's first university in 1893. One Hundred years later (July 1, 1994), the Montana Board of Regents of Higher Education restructured the state's public colleges and universities, with the goal of streamlining the state's higher education. It now has sixteen campuses divided among the two state university systems, and community colleges as follows:

The University of Montana System
University of Montana (flagship campus, in Missoula)
Missoula College University of Montana (in Missoula)
University of Montana Western (in Dillon)
Montana Technological University (in Butte)
Highlands College of Montana Tech (in Butte)
Helena College University of Montana (in Helena)
Bitterroot College University of Montana (in Hamilton)

Montana State University System
Montana State University (flagship campus, in Bozeman)
Gallatin College Montana State University (in Bozeman)
Montana State University Billings (in Billings)
City College at Montana State University Billings (in Billings)
Montana State University–Northern (in Havre)
Great Falls College Montana State University (in Great Falls)

Community Colleges
Dawson Community College (in Glendive)
Flathead Valley Community College (in Kalispell)
Miles Community College (in Miles City)

In addition to these 16 campuses Montana has three private colleges: Carroll College in Helena, Rocky Mountain College in Billings and University of Providence in Great Falls. Along with the U.S. Forest Service headquarters founded in 1908, lumber and the university remained the basis of the local economy for the next 100 years. The University of Montana enrollment for fall semester in 2020 was 10,015 students. The University is known for its law school, forestry school and business school.

A picture of my Monte Dolack
(a well-known graphic artist with a gallery in Missoula)
print of the Main Hall

As a matter of fact, the business school was the reason I was living in Missoula with my ex-husband and children in 1964. In addition to him, Pat Campbell, his sister and her husband, Maureen and Dick Ford, my sister's ex-husband and son, John and Mark Smith, and myself, have all graduated from U. of M. Another very important Missoula memory is the birth of my third child and second son, Mitch Campbell. He was born at St. Patrick's Hospital on April 1, which is commonly known as April Fool's Day. The effective day for the insurance to cover the expenses of his birth was April 1, and he was born on April 1. Before the end of that day I received a phone call from Human Resources saying that because he was born right on the effective date it would not be covered, very short pause, followed by "April Fools!" Yikes. Indelible memory added to a very special memory. Although Mitch only lived in Montana until he was in the 6th grade following are his feelings about the state:

"What Does Montana Mean to Me?

Montana is an old and dear friend – one of my longest and best of friends. More than that, Montana is part of me – just like my bones/blood or personality/philosophies. It's part of the story of who I am.

I can take a breath and see her mountain peaks and flowing streams. I can take a step and feel her pristine air go into my lungs. I can listen to a song and hear her crackling summer thunder. I think of her often and miss her when she's away..

No matter how long I've been away from her, though, she's always just a thought, just a moment away. With that, the feelings come rushing back. The Montana feelings – I couldn't make those sweet, wonderful feelings go away even if I wanted to.

But I don't want them to go away . . . keep them coming.

Long live Montana – just as I know her."

Another St. Patrick's Hospital memory involves a phone call stating that my fifth child and youngest daughter, Kori Campbell, who was living in Missoula at the time, had been admitted with severe hypothermia. Her father, all five siblings and myself immediately flew to Missoula to find her lying in a hospital bed with tubes and bandages, and a prognosis of "don't know how much of her hands or fingers she will lose, but she will survive." She did and only lost to the second joint on the little finger of her left hand. It probably doesn't make showing off her wedding ring optimum, but she is very much alive today.

The 2020 United States Census shows Missoula's population at 73,489, making it second only to Billings as largest city in Montana. Missoula is approximately 10 miles south of the boundary for the Flathead Indian Reservation.

Arlee is noted in the Flathead Indian Reservation

St. Ignatius is noted in the Flathead Indian Reservation.

Ronan (Pronounced Row-NAN) is about 385 miles from my cabin on the Stillwater River that is considered to be in Nye, Montana.

Ronan is on the Flathead Indian Reservation and has a population of 1,955 people. It was established in 1894 and was originally called Spring Creek, but was later named for Major Peter Ronan who wrote a history of the Flathead Indians and was the first Flathead Indian agent. Once we got to Ronan, after a long day in the motor home, we could relax and venture out from our comfortable setting in Holli's cousin's yard, only when ready.

Ronan is only 14 miles from Polson which is on the southern shore of **Flathead Lake,** so let's talk about the largest lake in Montana, and as already stated, the largest fresh water lake west of the Mississippi. It covers 197 square miles, has a maximum depth of 370 feet, and is a good place to catch rainbow, brown or brook trout and largemouth or smallmouth bass. It's also wonderful for boating, if you catch it on a clear, no storms brewing, day. A friend of mine who lived on Flathead Lake for 20 years said they had two sayings: (1) "If it's a beautiful day, drop everything and get out on the water," and (2) "If you are on the water and see a storm coming, get off the water and get off fast." Flathead is so big that it creates its own weather system and has many attributes of the ocean. There are also opportunities for hikers at Flathead Lake by boating to one of the following Islands: Wild Horse, Cromwell, Dream, Melita, Cedar, Bird, Mother-in-Law, Bull or Shelter. We were unable to get out on the water this trip, but I've been there before and it's the best.

Conversely, one of the smaller lakes, if not the smallest, in Montana is Echo Lake, about 14 miles from Flathead. It covers only

695 acres and is 80 feet deep. Motorized vehicles are not even allowed on this lake. (As a point of interest, Wikipedia lists lakes by county, of which there are 56 in Montana, with Petroleum County having the fewest lakes at six, which at a minimum gives Montana 336 lakes. But then there is Lake County having the most lakes at 80. So, long story short, Montana has a lot of lakes!) When I first moved to the Flathead area, Echo was the lake I wanted to live on. That didn't work out but living on Flathead Lake did, Woods Bay to be exact. I absolutely loved it there. My second favorite, ever home. A very close second to, if not a tie with, my present home on the Stillwater River in Nye, Montana.

East Shore of Flathead Lake

I was still living in California when we purchased the house on Woods Bay of Flathead Lake, considered to be in **Bigfork**. One of the first "small town" stories that my children and I laughed about was when I called the Bigfork Post Office to inquire what my address was going to be after the move. First off, they answered the phone. What a shock. That didn't happen in California. Next, the man who answered said something like: "Oh, you're the lady from California. We've heard all about you. Your address is Woods Bay. Just Woods Bay." Another of those stories was a result of a friend and I going into the Department of Motor Vehicles in Kalispell, (a town of about 12,000 about 18 miles northwest of Bigfork) to change the name on my driver's license secondary to my divorce. The two of us walked into a very empty room. I think there was one other person ahead of us and two clerks at the counter. When we got to the counter and exchanged our greetings one of the clerks said, "Whew, we have just been so busy." Really. You should try working at the DMV in California. From the time the door opens in the morning until it closes at night there is a steady stream of people, and some of them not so hospitable.

And now for my wonderful Woods Bay eagle story. My house was right on the water. I was standing on the front deck looking out over the bay. In the distance I could see what looked like an eagle standing on the water. As uninformed as I am, I was sure they couldn't do that. Soon it became apparent that it was standing on something white, maybe a piece of wood. I continued to watch as the eagle standing on the white object floated closer and closer to my dock. Suddenly the eagle flew off, and the white object lifted its head slightly, but didn't move anything else, continuing to float toward the shore. At that point I noticed that there were many ducks gathering around, both in the water and on the shore. It was a duck that had almost been drowned by the eagle but was recovering and the other ducks were escorting it in. A local, very good, friend of mine said that was routine for the eagles; hold the ducks head under water until it drowns and then fly away with the duck in its talons. What a privilege to witness one of nature's rituals. Another time, when this same friend and I were driving around the countryside we were able to observe an owl sitting on a fence post, not more than 20 feet away. Those are the wonders of Montana that never cease to impress me.

Bigfork is about 412 miles from my cabin on the Stillwater River that is considered to be in Nye, Montana.

Bigfork got its name from its location on a fork where the Swan River and Flathead River flow into Flathead Lake. As early as

1885, Everit L. Sliter set out 500 apple, cherry, plum, and pear trees on Flathead Lake's east shore. He became the first postmaster in 1901 and the east shore of Flathead Lake has been known for its fruit, mostly cherries, for years. The town has been described as: "A huddle of little grey houses in a hollow just below the dam and powerhouse" that supplies electricity for Kalispell and much of Flathead country. I'm assuming the electricity part is still true, but I can't believe that the "huddle of little grey houses" would still be included in any description of Bigfork today. It has transformed into a tourist destination offering outstanding productions in its summer playhouse (many of which I have enjoyed over the years and was very disappointed that the timing was not going to make it possible again this year), the Bigfork Inn as a preferred place to eat (with live music and dancing on the weekends – I hope they still have it), many art galleries and unique retail shops, and a local brewery. Current population 4,668. (In the good old days, when I lived there, they had a contest every year for artists to create a painting of Bigfork at Christmas, the winner to be used as that year's Bigfork Christmas card. I had a collection of those cards at one time. My very good friend won the contest one year with a photograph of the Swan River Bridge, which was about 100 yards from her home on the Swan River. That was the only year that a photograph was allowed in the contest.)

Native American Proverbs

BEWARE OF THE MAN WHO DOES NOT TALK AND THE DOG THAT DOES NOT BARK.

ALL DANGER DOES NOT COME WITH A WARNING.

"Everything on the earth has a purpose, every disease an herb to cure it, and every person a mission. This is the 'Indian' theory of existence."
— Mourning Dove (Christine Quintasket) - Salish Indian

(Mourning Dove was the pen name of Christine Quintasket, an Interior Salish woman who collected tribal stories among Northern Plateau peoples in the early twentieth century. She described centuries-old traditions with the authority of first-hand knowledge)

Salish Chief Charlo was the son of Chief Victor, who was the son of Chief Three Eagles who met with Lewis and Clark in 1805. Chief Charlo fell heir, not only to the tribal leadership, but also to his father's struggle to retain the rights of the tribe to their ancestral homeland, their dearly loved Bitter Root Valley. Charlo was Chief when his people were forced to make the move from the Bitter Root Valley to the Flathead Reservation. Chief Charlo led his people away from their homeland, sitting erect on his pony, he never looked back, nor would he ever talk about the Bitter Root Valley, nor his life there. He died a bitter man, feeling responsible for his people and felt that he had let them down.

Kootenai Chief Abraham was the son of Chief Thomas Blind (because he was), who was the son of Chief Three Moons (Little Big Blanket). Chief Abraham was the most respected and influential chief since the arrival of non-Indians in the Kootenai Valley. He is said to have offered seven horses in trade for the first house cat brought to the ferry, because he thought it was a tame cougar.

The **Flathead Indian Reservation** was established by treaty in 1855 and covers almost two thousand square miles of land, including a large portion of **Flathead Lake**. This reservation is home to the Salish (Sqelixw – Bitterroot/Pend d'Oreille) and Kootenai (pronounced KOO tun ee) ('aqtsmaknik) people. Population of the reservation is 26,829. The Indians of this area were named Flathead by Europeans who came to the area. The name was originally applied to various Salish peoples, based on the practice of artificial cranial deformation by some of the groups, though the modern groups associated with the Flathead Reservation never engaged in that practice. There are 26 communities on the reservation, the most of any reservation in Montana.

Towns on the Reservation:

Arlee was named after Alee, a Salish chief. The spelling with an 'r' is peculiar to English as the Indian word, which means 'red night' has no 'r.' In fact, there is no 'r' in the Indian alphabet. Arlee has a population of 641 people and is home to the Garden of 1,000 Buddhas. The garden was founded by Gochen Tulku Sang-ngag Rinpoche, a Tibetan master of the Nyingma school of Buddhism. Following a traditional Buddhist method, Sang-Ngag claimed to have chosen the location immediately upon seeing it, recalling a prophetic dream from his youth which corresponded to the garden's landscape. Subsequently, Sang-ngag's non-profit organization, *Ewam*, received the land in an anonymous donation by one of the Rinpoche's disciples, and construction began in 2000. (Arlee is only 30 miles from Ronan so it was an easy trip for us and a worthwhile one.)

1,000 Buddhas, Arlee, Montana

Bear Dance is located on Montana Highway 35 on the east bank of Flathead Lake. Population is 282 people.

Big Arm is situated on the south side of Big Arm, a large bay on Flathead Lake, hence its name. Population is 169 people. (I have a collection of statuettes, made of clay, approximately six inches in height, mostly Montana type people; i.e., Indians, cowboys, farmers. The first was a gift to me and was made by Kay Wearling. Years ago I went to Big Arm and met Val Knight, who is the daughter of Kay and who was then making the sculptures at her Val Knight Studio in Big Arm. Each statuette comes with an inscription, examples: "According to an old Indian proverb, He who once drinks of the waters of the North will always return to them," and "A cowgirl and her horse are one whether working cattle or having fun.")

Camas was named for the abundant camas plants, a member of the lily family with an onion-like flavor. The Salish and Kootenai Indians would come frequently to dig the bulbs as they were a staple in their diet. The current population is 73 people.

Charlo was originally called Big Flat, then Charlotte, and finally, in 1918, Charlo in honor of Chief Charlo. Current population is 286 people.

Dayton is on the shores of Flathead Lake and is the place of embarkment for boaters going to Wild Horse Island. Current population is 97 people.

Dixon was established under the name of Jocko City, but it was changed to Dixon in honor of Governor and Senator Joseph Dixon. Current population is 216 people.

Elmo was established in 1911 and has a current population of 165 people. (One of the very few, very special people in my life was Barbara Bennetts. She built a home in Elmo with the intention of retiring there. Unfortunately, those plans were cut short by cancer. She called me from her last hospital stay and we decided that I would come to see her in about two weeks after her two daughters, Bonnie and Stacie, had gone home. According to Bonnie, her mother died lying on her favorite couch, which she affectionately called "Naughy," in the living area of her newly constructed home, praying with her daughters and her ex-husband, Charlie.)

Evaro is located on the southernmost tip of the Flathead Indian Reservation, approximately 12 miles north of downtown Missoula and is served by US Highway 93. It has a population of 343 people. Evaro was named by Adna Anderson, a construction engineer for the railroad, possibly for a French count who had visited the area. A post office opened at Evaro in 1905.

Finley Point has a population of 413 people.

Hot Springs was founded in 1913 and was named for the natural hot springs in the area. It has a population of 558 people. (I have actually experienced sitting in one of those creeks where the hot water joins in.)

Jette has a population of 143 people.

Kerr has a population of 73 people.

Kicking Horse has a population of 43 people.

Kings Point has a population of 229 people.

Lindisfarne has a population of 409 people.

Lonepine was established in 1911 and has a population of 160 people.

Niarada was established in 1911 and has a population of 7. (Here we go again. Definitely smaller than the 19 of Ismay.)

Pablo was established in 1917 and was named for Michel Pablo, a Flathead chief and rancher and stockman, who, by raising bison, is one of the individuals responsible for saving them from extinction. Pablo is headquarters for the Indians on the Flathead Reservation and home to the Salish Kootenai College. It has a population of 2,274.

Polson lies on the southern shores of Flathead Lake. It was established in 1898 and was named for David Polson, a stockman who lived south of town. Polson has a population of 4,918 and hosts the Flathead Cherry Festival every year. (Another major event that we missed because of the timing of our tour.)

Ravalli is located at the junction of roads coming from Polson, Thompson Falls and Missoula. It was established in 1887 and was named for a Jesuit missionary, Father Antonio Ravalli. It had a population of 76 at the 2010 census.

Rocky Point has a population of 30 people.

St. Ignatius Mission is in the Mission Mountains of Montana

St. Ignatius is only 14 miles from Ronan which again enabled our ability to visit it on our "free of travel" day. It was named for and is the site of the **St. Ignatius Mission**, established by Father Pierre-Jean DeSmet, a Belgian Jesuit missionary, who worked for his entire career in the American Midwest and West. The mission was built in 1891 by American Indians and Jesuit missionaries and is listed on the National Register of Historic Places. The setting for this mission is one of the single most beautiful settings I have seen in my lifetime. (Saint Ignatius of Loyola, for whom the mission is named, was a Spanish Catholic priest and theologian, who, with Peter Faber and Francis Xavier, founded the religious order of the Society of Jesus -The Jesuits. Teaching and missionary work are the purposes of the Society of Jesus, who, as priests, are bound by a fourth (special) vow of obedience to the sovereign pontiff, to be ever-ready to fulfill the special missions of the papacy. St. Ignatius was canonized, receiving the title of Saint, in 1622. He is the patron saint of the Society of Jesus, all spiritual retreats and soldiers.)

Turtle Lake has a population of 318 people.

Seal for the Salish and Kootenai Tribes on Flathead Reservation

Towns between Ronan and Libby

Charlo is noted on the Flathead Indian Reservation.

Moiese (pronounced Moh EEZ) is near the National Bison Range and was named for an Indian subchief. Population 1,792.

Dixon is noted on the Flathead Indian Reservation.

Paradise is rumored to have come from "Pair o' Dice" which was the name of a local roadhouse. This was the spot where railway men traveling west changed their watches from Mountain Standard Time to Pacific Standard Time. Current population is 114.

Plains was originally Horse Plains as the Indians and their horses wintered there. Eventually, stockman from as far away as Walla Walla, Washington, drove their horses there for the winter and large numbers of wild horses came to the protected area also. The name was shortened to only Plains. Population is 1,019.

Thompson Falls was named for David Thompson, founder of the Northwest Fur Company and for the natural falls in the Clark Fork River. In 1883, 10,000 immigrants wintered in Thompson Falls on their way to the gold fields of Idaho. Twenty saloons were opened to accommodate them and they all made a profit. Population is 1,489.

Noxon, population 162, was established in 1883 as a Northern Pacific Railroad station.

Heron, population 281, is another Northern Pacific Railroad station and is almost on the Idaho border. According to something I read the Dixon to Heron route was supposed to be the most scenic drive in Montana. I disagree. It was lovely, but not any more so than West Yellowstone to Bozeman down the Gallatin or Polson to Bigfork around the east side of Flathead Lake.

Troy has a population of 972 people. Where the name came from is in dispute. One group says it was named by E. L. Preston, surveyor for the railroad, for the son of the family with whom he was boarding, Troy Morrow. Others say it was named for the Troy weight system, that was used for measuring gold, silver and other precious metals. Troy is at the lowest elevation, 1,800 feet, of any community in Montana.

Libby is 520 miles from my cabin on the Stillwater River that is considered to be in Nye, Montana.

Libby was named for a daughter of George Davis, an early settler. Miners flocked to Libby Creek in 1867. It was deserted by the 1870s. In 1892, with the arrival of the Great Northern Railway, the town moved downstream and the name was shortened from Libbysville to Libby. Current population is 2,758.

The Libby Dam

The **Libby Dam** is about 17 miles east of Libby and 45 miles south of Rexford. The dam was dedicated by President Gerald Ford in 1975. The reservoir created by the Libby Dam is **Lake Koocanusa,** the name created by combining the first three letters of <u>Koo</u>tenai River (named for Kootenai Indians), <u>Can</u>ada, and <u>USA.</u> The reservoir extends ninety miles behind the dam, 42 miles of which are in Canada. The **Koocanusa Bridge** which crosses the reservoir is the longest and highest bridge in Montana. With a length of 2,437 feet and standing 270 feet (depending on water levels) above the lake. This was one of the experiences I was so looking forward to and it did not disappoint. Just a bit scary to drive across and, oh so beautiful.

Koocanusa Bridge

Rexford is 62 miles north of Libby in the extreme northwest corner of Montana in Lincoln County. It is 12.5 miles from the Canadian border and adjacent to Idaho on the west. Rexford was established in 1901 with construction of the Great Northern Railway, but was not incorporated until 1966 in order to negotiate with the U.S. Army Corps of Engineers during construction of the Libby Dam. Current population is 123.

Rexford is the home of the oldest Montana Amish community that first settled there in 1974. It was from the Koocanusa Bichon Kennels, actually a couple belonging to this Amish community, that I purchased my two Bichon Frise puppies in 2015. Because the newborn puppies were so far from my home in Columbus, I was unable to pick them out myself so simply said I wanted the biggest male and female of the litter. Oops, the first litter had only males, but three days later a second litter had a female. So, eight weeks later, the Amish couple got a ride with a neighbor to Kalispell where I met them in the Wal-Mart parking lot and saw for the first time Kasper, born February 21, 2015, and Koko Rose, named after my Grandmother Rose, whose birthday she shares, February 24, 2015. These dogs have proven themselves to be the very best of companions for me. and I am forever grateful to the Amish couple from whom I purchased them. As an aside, all arrangements prior to actually meeting were done over the telephone, which was actually in the home of a neighbor, as Amish do not have phones, and that same neighbor had created and attended the website by which I learned of the dogs. (Sadly, since this writing they have both passed – not even eight years old. They were so loved and are deeply missed.)

Koko and Kasper (taken on their 7th birthday this year)

I had no opportunity to actually get to know the couple, and I don't even remember their names. I have recently tried to contact them using the same phone number as before, but it was reported as "no longer in service." I then tried to contact them by mail using the address to which I had sent the deposit check and that letter was returned as "undeliverable." So my hope of getting from them information about their Amish community has been squashed. Therefore, what follows is what I have learned from other sources.

There are five Amish communities in Montana at this time. Rexford was followed by two communities established in 1997, one in St. Ignatius, Lake County and one in the Ashland/Forsyth area, Rosebud County; one in Whitehall, Jefferson County in 2001 and the most recent in the Moore/Lewistown area, Fergus County in 2008. (And I have just recently been told there is a new Amish community in Roberts, Carbon County. In fact, the property owners of Midnight Canyon, where I live, have contracted with a member of the Roberts' Amish community to re-deck our Midnight Canyon Bridge.) As of the 2020 census, there are a total of 1,045 Amish in Montana.

According to an article on the Internet written by Jack Zavada dated July 22, 2018, to be Amish means:

"The Amish are among the most unusual Christian denominations, seemingly frozen in the 19th century. They isolate themselves from the rest of society, rejecting electricity, automobiles, and modern clothing. Although the Amish share many beliefs with evangelical Christians, they also hold to some unique doctrines. The Amish are one of the Anabaptist (which means they believe in baptism as adults not as children) denominations and number over 150,000 worldwide. They follow the teachings of Menno Simons, founder of the Mennonites, and the Mennonite *Dordrecht Confession of Faith*. In the late 17th century, this European movement split from the Mennonites under the leadership of Jakob Ammann, from whom they derive their name. The Amish became a reform group, settling in Switzerland and the southern Rhine River region. "Mostly farmers and craftsmen, many of the Amish migrated to the American colonies in the early 18th century. Because of its religious tolerance, many settled in Pennsylvania, where the largest concentration of Old Order Amish is found today."

Amish School in Rexford, Montana

Other Anabaptist religion based communities in Montana are Hutterites and Mennonites. They have roots dating back to the 16th century radical reformation. The Mennonites took their name from Frisian Menno Simons and split from the Amish in 1693. Today, the greatest differences between Amish and Mennonites stem mainly from practices rather than beliefs. Amish groups tend to shy away from technology and involvement with the greater world, by dressing "plain," using scooters and buggies for transportation, and remaining colonized. The Mennonites have embraced some of the world's technologies and stress the importance of missionary work, helping to spread their faith to over fifty countries around the world. In addition, they tend to live within the general population. They number about 500 in Montana today.

Mennonite Church

The Hutterites took their name from their founder Jakob Hutter who died in 1536. They maintain a communal lifestyle separate from the general population and number about 5,000 in Montana. There are several Hutterite colonies throughout Montana. The first was established in 1935 near Lewistown and the second in 1945 in Grass Range. There have been many added since then: another near Lewistown in 1947; Valier, Conrad, and Choteau in 1948; another in Choteau in 1949; and Cut Bank and Sweetgrass in 1951.

Hutterite Colony

Towns between Libby and Glacier Park:

Marion is called Swan alternatively with Marion. Population is 1,041.

Kila is on Smith Lake and only a few miles from the north end of Flathead Lake. It was originally called Sedan, but when William Kiley applied for the post office he asked for the name Kiley. However, the post office changed it to Kila. Population is 411.

Kalispell is a Salish word meaning "flat land above the lake". The Indians called the Flathead Valley "The park between the mountains." Using his own capital, Charles Edward Conrad, a businessman and banker from Fort Benton formed the

Kalispell Townsite Company with three other men, circa 1890. Conrad built a large mansion in 1895 which is available to the public for tours today. This mansion put me in mind of the Moss Mansion in Billings, but the Conrad Manson is much more elegant and on grounds that are spectacular. Kalispell is 17 miles from the Big Mountain Ski area in Whitefish, 7 miles from Flathead Lake, 31 miles from Glacier Park and 22 miles from Hungry Horse Dam. It is in an awesomely beautiful location. Population is 23,935.

Columbia Falls original townsite was planned for a palace near a waterfall on the Flathead River which is a part of the headwaters of the Columbia River – thus the name. Prior to that it had been called Monaco. There are currently 5,651 residents of Columbia Falls, one of whom created a beautiful water color painting for me. It was in the 1990's when I was living in Big Fork that I saw some drawings she had done of the "Precious Moments" children. I collected nativities at the time, so I asked her if she could paint a nativity using the "Campbell Soup Kids" as the characters, paralleling my own children who are Campbells. She did indeed, replicating the various hair colors and body statures. A friend of mine had it elegantly framed for me. I still have it and I still love it.

Hungry Horse sprang up during the construction of **Hungry Horse Dam** when the U.S. Bureau of Reclamation placed more than one hundred prefabricated buildings at the site to house workers. In 1948, Flathead County commissioners changed the name of the newly formed "Damtown" to Hungry Horse. The name comes from a local legend about two horses, Tex and Jerry, that escaped and almost starved to death in deep snow along the South Fork of the Flathead River. Construction of the dam was started in 1944 and completed on July 18, 1953. At a ceremony on October 1, 1952, President Harry S. Truman threw a switch to start power generation. The dam site is in a deep, narrow canyon. **Hungry Horse Reservoir** is located high in the Rocky Mountains, less than 30 miles from the Continental Divide and is surrounded by more than 25 mountain peaks. The reservoir is about 34 miles long and 23,800 acres and offers excellent opportunities for fishing, boating, water skiing, and swimming. Available fish species are cutthroat trout, bull trout, and whitefish. The surrounding mountains are popular big game hunting areas and several of the small tributaries have their headwaters in nearby alpine lakes. The area is managed by the Flathead National Forest. Camping there for two nights was absolutely delightful. So very beautiful.

Hungry Horse Dam

Coram was called Coram Nyack as a station on the Great Northern Railroad. Population is 302.

West Glacier is the western entrance to Glacier National Park, hence the name. It was originally called Belton. Population is 124.

Glacier National Park, which is wholly in Montana, was created by President William Howard Taft in 1910 on land inhabited by the Blackfeet Indians until their removal to an adjacent reservation. It was named Glacier because the mountains were formed by glaciers during an ice age and there were 60 existing

glaciers in 1910. According to a Public Broadcasting System (PBS) documentary, a glacier is defined as ice that is moving, a minimum of 25 acres of ice.

Construction on the Glacier Park Hotel began in 1912. The massive logs were brought from Seattle via the railroad. They were so large that there could be no more than three per train car. The price of building the hotel was shared between the railroad and the park service with the railroad spending by far the most. The hotel was completed June 15, 1913.

Another important goal toward making the new park accessible to the general public was to create a road through it. This became a Herculean task because of the treacherous terrain. As a result, there was a great turnover of men. One hundred and twenty five men came and went just surveying for the road. They started the actual work with picks and shovels and lots of dynamite, with 300 men working at the peak, three of whom died in the process. The crews were almost exclusively determined by nationality, speaking their native language and being led by one of their own. The Italian crews did all the masonry work building the retaining walls, of which there are approximately seventeen. It took four summers to complete the road, and it officially received its name, "The Going to the Sun Road," during the 1933 dedication. The road borrowed its name from nearby Going-to-the-Sun Mountain. Local legend and a 1933 press release issued by the Department of the Interior, told the story of the deity, Sour Spirit, who came down from the sun to teach Blackfeet braves the rudiments of the hunt. On his way back to the sun, Sour Spirit had his image reproduced on the top of the mountain for inspiration to the Blackfeet. An alternate story suggests a white explorer in the 1880s concocted the name and the legend. No matter which version is accurate, the road named "Going-to-the-Sun" still inspires all who travel it, and it is considered a civil engineering landmark.

President Franklin Delano Roosevelt toured Glacier Park in 1934. The park had acquired six 1927 Cadillacs to accommodate him and his entourage. This provided the seed for the future investment in buses to provide tours for the general public. President Roosevelt gave his August 5, 1934, radio address from Glacier National Park.

"Gear Jammer" bus in Glacier Park

An iconic feature of Glacier National Park is the "gear jammer" buses. They were originally purchased from the White Motor Company in 1936, had manual transmissions and, therefore, were known to have their gears ground by the drivers maneuvering up the Going to the Sun Road. Hence the name. In 2002, they were all restored by Ford Motor Company, including being switched to automatic transmissions, but the name remains. The red color was determined by matching paint to the Mountain Ashberry.

Glacier Park is a "must see" for everybody. The mountains are more marvelous than the Swiss Alps. The animals are wonderous, when you are lucky enough to see them. The "gear jammer" tour is lots of fun and you learn a lot from the driver.

The Bob Marshall Wilderness is just south of Glacier National Park. It is nicknamed "The Bob" by locals and Forest Service personnel, and was named after Bob Marshall (1901-1939) who was a forester in the federal government, conservationist, and co-founder of The Wilderness Society. The Bob is the fifth largest wilderness in the lower 48 with 1,009,356 acres. (Wilderness areas are established by Congress under the Wilderness Act of 1964. This designation means that the area has to be left as it is found – no roads or additional structures.) According to Wikipedia: "The Bob ranges in altitudes of 4,000 to more than 9,000 feet. With numerous waterfalls, lakes, and dense forests, the wilderness is prime Grizzly bear habitat. The U.S. Forest

Service claims that the population density of this species is higher in The Bob than can be found anywhere else in the U.S., outside of the Greater Yellowstone Ecosystem or Alaska. The Bob is also home to many other large mammals, such as moose, elk, black bear, mountain goat, bighorn sheep, wolverine, cougar, Canadian lynx, and wolf. Bald eagles, osprey, pelican, and trumpeter swan are just a few of the bird species found. The dense old-growth forests are dominated by Douglas fir, arch, and spruce. Forest fires have changed large areas in the wilderness complex in recent years. Wilderness areas do not allow motorized or mechanical equipment, including bicycles and hang gliders. Camping and fishing are allowed; fishing requires a state license. There are no roads and there is no logging or mining, in compliance with the Wilderness Act. Some administrative cabins constructed in the early 1920s afford refuge for trail crews and wilderness rangers. Wilderness areas within National Forests and Bureau of Land Management areas allow hunting in season."

My youngest child and fourth son, Mason Campbell, has an up close and personal experience with The Bob and I'm going to let him tell you about it in his own words.

"Being born in Montana and moving to California at the age of five our household was filled with the romantic notion of how beautiful and simple life is in Montana. I would often listen to stories that my parents and older siblings (I am the youngest of six) told of this almost idyllic place, a perfect mixture of beauty and peace. What would always stick out to me during these stories was the sky that blanketed the state as a warm, starry blanket that provided a sense of comfort to my family. I too wanted to experience the 'Big Sky' of Montana, not through the stories any longer but for myself. I did not know how or when that would become a reality, but I knew one day I wanted to experience sleeping under the big sky of Montana.

"As a sixteen-year-old, troubled youth growing up in California, I turned away from the family in general and specifically this misplaced notion that Montana is a place to find peace, serenity, and a sense of belonging. I did not want to belong to anyone or anything, especially this crazy love and admiration my family has for Montana. My family held an intervention, I was sent to Montana to be a part of The Wilderness Treatment program, on a working farm outside of Kalispell. As part of the program each person goes on a two-three week back-packing trip through the Bob Marshall wilderness. As a troubled youth, who wanted to distance himself from his family or any adult authority figure, I was angry and unwilling to look inside myself and acknowledge I am responsible for my own actions and behaviors. It was simply easier to blame other people. So, that is what I did, saying things like, they do not know me, they cannot understand me, I'm different, I'm special, I'm the center of the universe.

"It is time to go to the Bob Marshall for a three-week backpacking trip. It was through this experience, back-packing in the majestic Montana wilderness that my entire perspective changed. I would like to say that for every step I took and every glance I made at the extraordinary landscape I immediately gained wisdom. After all, I am just another person in this big, beautiful world and want to be a part of something that is bigger than myself too. However, every step and every glance were met with frustration and spitefulness of why are we doing this? This is so dumb, it is not going to help anything. After a week of hiking with a 50-pound pack on my back, breaking down camp, setting up camp, it was time, as the adult authority figures announced, 'for your solos gentlemen.' A solo is where you spend three days, completely on your own, no other human contact and whatever you do is completely your choice. Finally, I am in charge of me and finally I get to be away from these other people who don't get me. The first night of my solo, I did not put up a tent, I did not prepare my campsite, I didn't organize, I did nothing as a big middle finger to all who were in change. I do not need your guidance or you, I will do this exactly my way. As I laid in my sleeping bag, I began to notice how big is the Montana sky and, as I began to trace the sky from one end to the other an uncontrollable feeling of warmth, love, and belonging came over me and I laid there and cried thinking about my family. It was the big sky of Montana that wrapped its arms around me in the Bob Marshall wilderness when I was in my most vulnerable state, and provided me with a sense of comfort, peace and appreciation.

"As I woke the next morning with a new sense of pride and appreciation for myself and the world around me, I immediately began to set up my tent, organize my gear and clean up my campsite, so any visitors would feel welcomed. I spent the next two days, gathering wood, searching for edible berries (mission unsuccessful), bathing and playing in a nearby creek, reading the Alcoholics Anonymous book, memorizing The Serenity Prayer (God, grant me the serenity to accept the things I cannot change, courage to change the things I can and the wisdom to know the difference) and going on mini adventures/scavenger hunts to collect anything to add to the appeal of my new home, such as pine cones, rocks, sticks or whatever trinkets The Bob provides. At the end of my stay, I saw a counselor approaching my campsite which brought a big smile to my face. With a sense of pride and newfound appreciation in my heart, I was eagerly awaiting his words as I had imagined them for the last two days. I gave the counselor a big hug and his words felt like poetry as they traveled from my ears to my heart; 'you have made the most of this incredible journey and have begun the lifelong transition of looking inward to love yourself, which allows you to love others. I could not be prouder of you.' The Bob Marshall wilderness, the Big Sky of Montana and a solo for 3 days gave me new perspective, strength, and humility to replace my inner darkness with an inner light. I AM FOREVER GRATEFUL" (A brief explanation of how the solos worked: counselors would station each boy in an area that they could oversee each and every move they made, so any possible dangers could be intercepted.)

Towns between Glacier Park and Cut Bank:

St. Mary had an on-again, off-again post office starting in 1898 to its final closing in 1915. It is on the western border of the Blackfeet Indian Reservation, adjacent to Glacier National Park and the eastern terminus of the Going-to-the-Sun Road. Fewer than 50 people reside in the village year-round; however, the population increases tenfold on a busy summer evening. Several lodges, restaurants and cafés, a small grocery store, two gas stations and campgrounds are located in the village.

Browning is noted in the Blackfeet Indian Reservation.

Cut Bank is about 347 miles from my cabin on the Stillwater River that is considered to be in Nye, Montana.

Cut Bank was named for a deep gorge nearby that was made by Cut Bank Creek. The Blackfeet Indians had described the stream that runs through this area as: "The river that cuts into the white clay banks." The population of Cut Bank jumped from less than one thousand to over four thousand in 1960 when oil and gas was discovered and continued to produce. Current population is 3,056.

Cut Bank is the home of Frank Jarvenpaa, our personal driver on this trip and the husband of Holli and son-in-law of my sister. It was his former farm/ranch where we parked our motor home for one night. Following are his comments:

"I grew up in Cut Bank in the 1960's and 1970's about five miles west of Cut Bank on the Blackfeet Indian Reservation along the Cut Bank Creek, which was more like a small river that carved a 100 foot deep canyon through the middle of our 1,200-acre farm/ranch. (Farm is property used to raise crops and ranch is property used to raise livestock.) Our buildings were about 100 yards from the creek in the same location as an old Blackfeet camp that included a buffalo jump (A cliff formation which Indigenous peoples of North America historically used to hunt and kill plains bison in mass quantities.) and rock lookout. I've always lived in Montana. My current home for the past 20 years is five miles south of Roberts on the Rock Creek. We are part of my wife's family cabin on the Stillwater River. My career as an electrical engineer in the power industry was in Billings, which is on the Yellowstone River. A river of some sort has always run through me." (Pause to let that sink in....)

"Cut Bank was a mix of ranchers, farmers, oil field 'rough necks' (A term for a person whose occupation is hard manual labor. The term applies across a number of industries, but is most commonly associated with the workers on a drilling rig.), Blackfeet Indians and a couple of large German Hutterite Colonies. It borders the Blackfeet Reservation, which extends west to Browning and Glacier Park. Probably the majority of the Whites were of Scandinavian decent, including my Norwegian grandfather. Cut Bank was a hub of about 4,000 people with a robust main street and virtually every good and service needed. It had more bars than churches. However, I believe every Christian denomination of the times was represented. Meanwhile, it was common for the night to end with a brawl between the Whites and the Indians at one or more of the local bars.

"Cut Bank is the coldest spot in the continental US, according to weather data. The weather is extreme to say the least. It's hot and dry in the summer and temps as low as 50 degrees below zero in the winter. Winds literally blew freight trains off the tracks near Browning. Glacier County is not for the 'faint of heart'. Most people worked out in the elements in the oil patch, farms and ranches. As a lineman for the Rural Electric Coop, my father would often get called in the middle of a stormy night to come to the rescue to help restore power and heat somewhere in the county. These storms often required him to climb to the top of a 30-foot power pole with hooks and a belt to make repairs while swinging in blizzard winds. Everyone had a head bolt heater or tank heater (the most common type of block heater is an electric heating element in the engine block, which is connected through a power cord often routed through the vehicle's grille.) on their vehicle engine and plugged it in to an electrical outlet at their house or place of work. Otherwise, you might not get it started again until the next big thaw, or 'Chinook', which would suddenly bring a gentle warm wind of 50 or 60 degrees Fahrenheit off the east face of the Rockies. I recall experiencing 60 to 100 degree temperature swings within a few hours during the dead of winter. It would last about a day and then turn cold again. My Irish/Polish grandmother described Cut Bank as 'colder than a well digger's ass'. Why would anyone choose to live here? In one word, 'opportunity' during those times. The glacial till soils were fertile and the oil and natural gas fields were productive, but the weather was harsh!

"My memories include:
- Dad taking me ice skating and ice fishing on the creek. (Pronounced 'crick', by Montanans.)
- Mom teaching me how to ride our horses bareback (no saddle) and how to swim in the river's current.
- Learning to drive our 1946 Chevy truck at the age of 8 so that I could drive it while Dad threw fresh straw bales from the field up for Mom to stack. Hang on Mom!

- The Blackfeet Indian's jovial wit, humor and family value of their elders. These Blackfeet would share anything with you and us with them as long as we treated each other respectfully.

- Putting tire chains on the pickup as soon as we turned off the highway and then taking them off again when we got back to the highway. This was the norm most of winter and spring for us. When things finally dried up, it was a big treat to take the family car to town for the first time in months. Most of the tires we purchased were steel studded snow tires, which are spectacular on icy roads.

- Spinning brodies (circles) with my friends in the family car on an ice-covered lake, once it got several feet thick.

- Chopping a hole in the deep ice of the creek every day so our cows could walk out and find drinking water. Spring ice jams with chunks the size of a vehicle that created 30 to 40 feet deep piles near our home.

- Searching for one or more missing Black Angus cows during calving season to see where they were about to give birth, in some deep sheltered coulee. Then bringing them a nice bed of hay and straw for mama and calf until the calf was strong enough to lead back to the main herd.

- Ferdinand the bull knew the perimeter of our ranch and would nudge his herd home. Ferdinand was a great help to our fencing requirements.

- Shooting gophers (prairie dogs) that damaged our crops.
- Mom cooking T-bone steaks for breakfast with fried trout eggs that Dad and I brought home during spawning season (when fish drop their eggs to be fertilized). My favorite meal was (and still is) beef Sweet Breads, browned and baked. This is the thymus gland from the cow.
- Cleaning dirt out of every orifice of my body at the end of a hot windy day in the fields. Often, we ended the day with a family swim at the creek in our favorite hole and basked on a large shale rock with a cold beer.
- Treasure hunting our buffalo jump and any old homestead dump in a coulee that Dad discovered while patrolling the power lines in Glacier County. One such hunt was orchestrated by my Grandpa. He loaded us up in his '58 Cadillac and forged the Milk River into 'no man's land' along the Canadian border. Here was an abandoned homestead from the late 1800's or early 1900's. Only deep wagon ruts led to the home. It was obviously abandoned in haste and/or despair. Everything, and I mean everything, was still there. The dining table was still set with dishes, silverware and a very thick layer of dust. It was like these people evaporated. Every pane of glass of the home was still intact. Out of shear respect, we tried to not touch anything.
- Picnics on Memorial Day weekend in Glacier Park with homemade fried chicken and a drive to the top of Logan

Pass, which is the highest point on the Going to the Sun Road and right on the Continental Divide.

- Fourth of July rodeos and family holidays in Choteau (a town about 80 miles from Cut Bank).
- The Toole County Fair in Shelby (about 24 miles from Cut Bank), Indian Days in Browning (about 35 miles from Cut Bank), ski trips to Big Mountain and the Sky Slide in Great Falls. (a water slide that closed in 1977 in Great Falls that is about 105 miles from Cut Bank)

"For me, growing up in Cut Bank produced perseverance, self-sufficiency and endurance. Finlanders call this 'Sisu'. In addition, growing up on a farm/ranch produced compassion and a deep appreciation for blessings in disguise, God's love of humanity and all creatures on earth. Sadly, small town opportunities went by the way side via mega agriculture business and box stores. I was lucky enough to still carve out a good living in Montana and I am grateful. No matter where you've lived, there are few things you don't miss."

Blackfoot Indian Proverb
LIFE IS NOT SEPARATE FROM DEATH.
IT ONLY LOOKS THAT WAY.

"From nowhere we came; into nowhere we go. What is life? It is the flash of a firefly in the night. It is the breath of a buffalo in the wintertime. It is the little shadow which runs across the grass and loses itself in the sunset."
—Crowfoot Blackfoot Warrior Chief

(Chief Crowfoot was head chief of the Blackfoot people and a strong advocate of peace and accommodation with whites.)

The **Blackfeet Indian Reservation** is bordered by Canada on the north and Glacier National Park on the west. It was established by treaty in 1855 and is home to the Blackfeet (Niisitapi) Indians who are part of what is known as the Blackfoot Confederacy, which is made up of four separate bands: North Piegan (pronounced PEE-gun), South Piegan, Blood and Siksika. The reservation covers 3,000 square miles of land, and has a population of 17,321 people, making it one of the 10 largest tribes in the United States. The Blackfeet people have a spiritual and cultural connection to Glacier Park and consider the Rocky Mountain range to be the backbone of the world. The belief is that they got the name Blackfeet from the color of the moccasins they wore, made of leather, the soles of which were dyed or painted black. (Some Blackfoot people are annoyed by the plural "Blackfeet," which is obviously an Anglicization. But most Blackfoot people accept both terms. "Blackfoot" is more commonly used in Canada, and "Blackfeet" is more commonly used in the United States.)

Towns on the reservation:

Babb is the gateway to the Many Glacier area in Glacier Park, so it has a large influx of tourists during the summer. Its year-round population is 72. The town was named for C.C. Babb, district engineer in charge of the St. Mary's Irrigation Project. It has had a post office since 1905.

Browning is headquarters for the tribe and the only incorporated town on the reservation. It has a population of 940. The town was named in 1885 for Commissioner of Indian Affairs, Daniel M. Browning.

East Glacier Park Village has a population of 388. The Great Northern Railway platted the community of Midvale in the 1890s. The town name was eventually changed to Glacier Park and officially became East Glacier Park in 1949.

Heart Butte takes its name from the small heart shaped peak southwest of town. It has a population of 600.

Little Browning has a population of 206.

North Browning has population of 2,861.

St. Mary is the eastern terminus of the Going-to-the-Sun Road which bisects the park east to west. Its year around population is about 264 but it increases tenfold on a busy summer evening. U.S. Route 89 passes through the village, which lays between Saint Mary Lake in Glacier Park and Lower St. Mary Lake on the reservation, hence the name.

South Browning has a population of 1,600.

Starr School has a population of 329

Seal of the Blackfeet Indian Reservation

Towns between Cut Bank and Great Falls

Valier was named for Peter Valier from LaCombre, Wisconsin, who supervised the building of the Montana Western Railroad. The Montana Western was only 22.2 miles long but important because it connected Valier with the Great Northern Railroad. Population is 546.

Brady is likely named for the Brady brothers. Charles A. Brady was a physician, who treated an outbreak of small pox in the area, and Thomas E. Brady, who was an attorney. Current population is 74. (When I was traveling in 2013 on a "Fall Foliage" bus tour, there was a couple on the tour from Brady, Montana. I happen to have a grandson named Brady, so I asked if they could provide me with something that had Brady, Montana, on it to give to my grandson. The only thing they could find for me was a spaghetti strap, woman's top, from "Dusty's First Annual Bike Rodeo," held in 2011 and sponsored by Dusty's Bar and Grill. Miracle of miracles, my daughter-in-law, Brady's mother, still has that top so you can see proof that there is a Brady Campbell and a Brady, Montana.)

Great Falls is about 240 miles from my cabin on the Stillwater River that is considered to be in Nye, Montana.

"**Great Falls** is named for a series of five waterfalls located on the Missouri River north and east of the city. The Lewis and Clark Expedition of 1805–1806 was forced to portage around a 10-mile stretch of the river in order to bypass the falls; the company spent 31 days in the area, performing arduous labor to make the portage. Three of the waterfalls, known as Black Eagle, Rainbow and the Great Falls (or the Big Falls), are among the sites of five hydroelectric dams in the area, giving the city its moniker, 'The Electric City.' Other nicknames for Great Falls include 'The River City' and 'Western Art Capital of the World.' The founding of Great Falls was the brainchild of Paris Gibson, a Maine-born entrepreneur who became acquainted with railroad magnate James J. Hill in Minneapolis, Minnesota. By the 1880s, Gibson was a sheep man in Fort Benton, Montana. He visited the Great Falls of the Missouri River in 1880 and was deeply impressed by the possibilities for building a major industrial city near the falls with power provided by hydroelectricity. He returned in 1883 with friend Robert Vaughn and some surveyors and platted a permanent settlement on the south side of the river. The city's first citizen, Silas Beachley, arrived later that year. With investments from Hill and from Helena businessman Charles Arthur Broadwater, houses, a store, and a flour mill were established in 1884. The Great Falls post office was established on July 10, 1884, and Gibson was named the first postmaster... Great Falls was incorporated on November 28, 1888...'' according to Wikipedia. It is the home of two military installations; Malmstrom Air Force Base east of the city, and the Montana Air National Guard to the west, adjacent to the Great Falls International Airport. Great Falls is also home to the C.M.

Russell Museum devoted to the artist known for images of the American West. Current city population is 58,835. All of the waterfalls are truly magnificent and the interpretive center is wonderful, giving you everything you ever wanted to know about Merriweather Lewis and William Clark.

My only, and very minimal, personal connection with Great Falls, goes back many years, when I was a Freshman in high school. I had just joined an organization for young girls called Job's Daughters and was excited to attend a gathering in Great Falls. Memories are sketchy but include staying in the home of a girl a couple of years older who played a beautiful grand piano in the main area of the house. Her name was Nina, and she was something of a spitfire – to the mind of a very naïve young girl. Also, I was recently reminded that my then husband and I chaperoned our daughter and some of her friends to a basketball tournament in Great Falls. Not much there, I know, but Great Falls is a town for which I had no warm and fuzzy, or of any other texture, of feelings/memories. Maybe this tour has changed that a tad.

Giant Springs is one of the largest freshwater springs in the county, producing over 156 million gallons of water each day, which flow into the Roe River. Giant Springs State Park provides excellent fishing opportunities along the Missouri River as well as a separate fishing pond. There are 30+ miles of paved and dirt single-track trails, which range in difficulty from beginner to expert for walking, running and hiking. The trails are all part of the larger **River's Edge Trail** System, which consists of nearly 60 miles of trail around the Great Falls area. The four Missouri River waterfalls (five, if you count the now buried Colter Falls) are all located within the park.

Giant Springs State Park

First Peoples Buffalo Jump State Park is an archaeological site believed to be the largest bison cliff jump in North America. Native peoples used this site for at least two thousand years prior to Lewis and Clark's expedition through Montana. The kill site consists of a mile long sandstone cliff; there are remnants of drive lines on top of the cliff and there are up to 18 ft. of compacted buffalo remains below the cliff. in an effort to pay homage to the buffalo and the people who honor this mighty animal, First Peoples Buffalo Jump State Park has an on-site education center. Of more than 300 bison kill sites in Montana, First Peoples Buffalo Jump is the first of its kind.

First Peoples Buffalo Jump State Park

A possible **Little Shell Reservation** in the future of Montana? According to a Visit Montana Publication, "Montana Explore Indian Country" the Little Shell Chippewa (Me'tis) gained state recognition from Montana in 2000 and are currently petitioning the federal government for federal status. Their tribal headquarters is GreatFalls which is the epicenter of the Little Shell programs. The Little Shell Tribe is the only state recognized tribe in Montana. Their language is a unique blend of native Chippewa, French, Cree and a little English. Their total enrollment is 4,500 members. (The Métis people originated in the

1700s when French and Scottish fur traders married aboriginal women, such as the Cree, and Anishinabe (Ojibway). Their descendants formed a distinct culture, collective consciousness and nationhood in the Northwest. See the Lewistown notes for more on the Metis people.)

Towns between Great Falls and Helena

Ulm is 12 miles southwest of Great Falls. It was named for William Ulm who had a ranch there which encompassed the townsite. Current population is 750.

Cascade was named for the "cascade" or "falls" of the Missouri River, though it's not very close to them. It was originally called Dodge then changed to Cascade in 1887. Charlie Russell lived there for awhile. Population is 648.

Craig has 16 people living there today. (Jere we have another town below the Ismay mark of 19.) It was named for Warren Craig a pioneer resident. It is said the original name was Stickney, after Benjamin Stickney, but in truth Stickney was on the other side of the Missouri River. The post office went back and forth between the two settlements until 1888 when it went permanently to Craig. The Craig post office was closed in 1953.

Wolf Creek has a population of 560 people. The name Wolf Creek came from a large creek that flows by it and is derived from the Indian phrase: "Creek Where The Wolf Jumped Too or To or In." The final word different depending on the source. It was first called Carterville.

Helena is about 225 miles from my cabin on the Stillwater River that is considered to be in Nye, Montana.

Helena (pronounced HEL-e-na) came into existence as a result of gold being discovered in Last Chance Gulch in 1864. A meeting was held to determine a new name for the rapidly expanding camp, thinking that Last Chance Gulch was not dignified enough. John Somerville spoke the loudest and talked the people into using the name of his home town in Minnesota, Helena (pronounced Hel-E-na). However, the people didn't like the way it was pronounced, so they adopted the HEL-e-na pronunciation, which stuck. The town boomed with the discovery of silver and lead, in addition to gold, and became the capital of the Montana territory in 1875. It was incorporated in 1881 and in 1889, when Montana became a state, the discussion immediately became whether or not it would remain the capital. Marcus Daly and his backers wanted Anaconda. William A. Clark wanted Helena. Obviously, Helena won. Ground was broken for the new capital buildings in 1898 and they were dedicated on July 4, 1902.

Montana State Capitol

A tour of this capitol is an absolute must. The architecture, the beauty, the many wonderful paintings, the history, all informative and a true source of pride for Montanans. We saw both houses of the legislature. The Senate has seats for its 50 members and the House for its 100 members. The seats in the senate gallery are the originals from 1902 and have an attached hat rack underneath as a place to put your cowboy hat. Actually, I was reminded of the time I was seated in the gallery of the House of Representatives to hear my very good friend give her first speech as a new representative from Helena, many, many years ago, early 1970's. And there he was again, Thomas Francis Meagher, a territorial governor of Montana, on his horse, on the front lawn, in bronze, larger than life. According to the guide, a gift from the Irish people of Butte to Montana.

The Original Governor's Mansion was built in 1888, which is one year before Montana became a state, by a William Chessman who owned a local water company. Therefore, it was not built as a home for Montana governors but as a home for the Chessman family, his wife and four daughters. The structure included a bathroom which was highly controversial at the time. When the mansion came up for sale in 1913 it was purchased by the state and became the Governor's Mansion. By then it had many improvements which included electricity and more bathrooms. That structure was home to Montana governors from 1913 to 1959 when a new home was built just two blocks from the capitol. Governor Hugo Aronson was its first inhabitant.

The **Cathedral of Saint Helena** is the cathedral of the Roman Catholic Diocese of Helena, Montana. Modeled by architect A.O. Von Herbulis after the Votivkirche in Vienna, Austria, the construction began on the cathedral in 1908, and held its first mass in November, 1914. Bishop John Patrick Carroll worked tirelessly to raise funds for building the cathedral and had an administrative role in management of the entire project. The cathedral sustained significant damage during the 1935 Helena earthquake, which required extensive renovations. It was added to the National Register of Historic Places in 1980. A cathedral is a church that has a bishop in charge of it and this cathedral is quite lovely.

St. Helena Cathedral, Helena, Montana

Due to the gold rush, Helena would become a wealthy city, with approximately 50 millionaires inhabiting the area by 1888, more per capita than in any city in the world. It is estimated about $3.6 billion in today's money was extracted from Helena during this period of time. The concentration of wealth contributed to the city's prominent, elaborate Victorian architecture.

Harrison Street Mansion in Helena

The Mansion District sits in the foothills of Mount Helena, in the city's southwest corner, and is home to streets like Lawrence, Monroe, Harrison, Madison and Dearborn. And, on one of those streets, Harrison, sits a mansion that was owned by my cousin, John Cadby and his wife Shirley from 1975 to 1996. The mansion they owned was one of the "sister" mansions; two sisters had identical mansions built, side by side, in 1895. The mansion John and Shirley purchased was three stories, with a total of 5,000 square feet. The third floor was a "ballroom" for dancing, with a small bedroom and bathroom for the "maid." They turned that floor into a "pool" room after receiving a pool table from my father, Eldon Shirley. The pool table had been purchased from a "going out of business" bar in some little berg between Billings and Roundup. The legend of the pool table was that Calamity Jane played pool on that table on her many trips through the area in pursuit of her romance with Wild Bill Hickok. Shirley stated, "It was magnificent living in that mansion. I would never have left it," and John stated, "We both miss Montana, but health matters won't permit us to live there."

In addition to the gold and silver and lead found in Helena are the gemstones found just outside of Helena. They include: jasper, garnet, varieties of quartz, rhodonite, serpentine, staurolite, topaz, tourmaline, and wonderstone. A few diamonds, diamond indicator minerals, and kimberlites have also been found in the state. According to the internet, "Montana is the only state in the United States with any significant production of gem-quality sapphires. There are four localities where sapphires are found in Montana, and only one of them is a primary deposit–the others are all alluvial deposits. The primary deposit is at Yogo Gulch (in the Judith Basin east of Helena), where extremely fine blue sapphires were first found when gold miners had blue pebbles turn up in their sluice boxes in the late 1860's. It wasn't until 1894, however, that they were recognized as valuable, when a sample was sent to George Kunz at Tiffany's in New York. .What made these sapphires so remarkable was their intense blue and violet colors and extremely high clarity. The original lamprophyre lava dike that was the source of the sapphires was located and subsequently mined from 1899 through roughly 1920, but production was low and the stones primarily small. Since that time there have been intermittent efforts at mining the Yogo sapphires, but larger supplies of sapphires from Sri Lanka, Thailand and elsewhere have made significant mining of these gems uneconomical–at least on a large scale.

Towns between Helena and Butte

Montana City, population 2,821, is located on top of one of the oldest prehistoric sites in the state of Montana. As early as 9,000 BC, Native Americans came to Montana City to collect chert, a rock similar to flint, which was used to make spear tips, arrowheads, and knives. White American explorers discovered gold at the site on July 2, 1862, and later that year U.S. Army Captain Jason L. Fisk brought a mule train from Minnesota, which stopped at the site and built the first houses that became Montana City. The town became one of the most important mining centers in Montana during the height of the gold rush in the 1860s. The Montana Town Company laid out the city in 1864, naming it after the territory's new name. Chinese miners took over from whites when the mines began to play out in 1868, and the town saw a brief revival after the arrival of the railroads and the establishment of a post office in the 1880s. At its height in the 1880s, Montana City had 3,000 residents and competed for the location of the state capital. Montana City was almost a ghost town for most of the 20th century until the Permanente Cement Company built a cement manufacturing plant there in 1940. Today, Montana City is a bedroom community serving Helena, which is only 7.5 miles away.

Clancy was named for the nearby Clancy Creek, which was named for a colorful old-timer known as "Judge" William Clancy. The original name was Prickly Pear until 1884, followed by Alhambra until 1947, and finally, Clancy. Current population is 1,964.

Jefferson City population is 596. It took its name from the nearby Jefferson River named for President Jefferson by Lewis and Clark.

Boulder was first called Boulder Valley, named for the massive stones strewn about the valley and was changed to just Boulder in 1897. The state schools for the deaf, blind and "feebleminded," now developmentally disabled, were established there in 1892. Three buildings in Boulder are listed on the National Register of Historic Places. Current population is 1,027.

Basin has a population is 267. It was founded in the Boulder River Basin, hence the name, by two miners, Lawson and Alport, in 1880. It is known for the radon mines in the area, which are considered by some to have health giving qualities.

(My very good friend, about whom I have referred in several of these sections, used to spend as much time as she could manage in the radon mines, in an effort to cure her cancer. Unfortunately it did not work.)

Butte is about 212 miles from my cabin on the Stillwater River that is considered to be in Nye, Montana.

Butte started out as Butte City, having been named by the miners after the sentinel-like peak called Big Butte, standing 6,369 feet above sea level. Gold was discovered there in 1864 followed by silver and copper. When Marcus Daly heard of the strikes he rushed from Nevada to Butte and discovered the richest vein of copper known. It was fifty feet wide. It took twenty years, but Mr. Daly became head of one of the most powerful monopolies, The Anaconda Copper Mining Company. By 1885 Butte had a population of 14,000 people and the copper boom was on. (Remember, Butte got the designation of Number One on their license plates because they were the most populous county – Silver Bow according to the 1930 census.) Population according to the 2020 census is 34,494, making it the fifth largest city in Montana today. Butte is the home of Montana Technological University (formerly Montana School of Mines) which is a premier STEM University: science, technology, engineering and mathematics. Student population for last year was 2,665.

Our Lady of the Rockies is a 90-foot statue built in the likeness of Mary, the mother of Jesus, that sits atop the Continental Divide overlooking Butte, Montana. It is the fourth-tallest statue in the United States after *Birth of the New World,* located on the Atlantic coastline in Puerto Rico, *The Statue of Liberty,* in New ork City, and the *Pegasus and Dragon.* In Hallandale Beach, Florida. The base is 8,510 feet above sea level and 3,500 feet above the town. The statue sits on private land and is lit and visible at night. The statue was originally conceived by Butte resident Bob O'Bill in 1979 as a tribute to the Virgin Mary following the recovery of his wife from cancer. Later, the statue was additionally dedicated to "all women, especially mothers." This statue can be seen easily from the interstate as you travel through Butte, but the only way to get up close and personal is via a tour bus. Don't miss it.

Our Lady of the Rockies, Butte, Montana

When we were in Butte all the locals were talking about the TV series that was being filmed there: a second prequel to 'Yellowstone,' titled "1923," starring Helen Mirren and Harrison Ford. It seems like the community was realizing considerable monetary profit as well as fascination with the process.

<u>Towns between Butte and Columbus</u>:

Three Forks, Logan, Manhattan, Belgrade, Bozeman, Livingston, Big Timber, Greycliff and Reed Point were all noted going the other direction.

"There are grander and more sublime land-scapes - to me. There are more compelling cul-tures. But what appeals to me about central Montana is that the combination of land-scape and lifestyle is the most compelling I've seen on this earth. Small mountain ranges and open prairie, and different weather, dif-ferent light, all within a 360-degree view."
- by Steve Abell, photographer

CENTRAL MONTANA + SOME ODDS AND ENDS

Lewistown is about 168 miles from my cabin on the Still-water River that is considered to be in Nye, Montana.

Lewistown is at the geographical center of Montana. It was first named Reed's Fort after Major A. S. Reed who opened the first post office in 1881. When the town was incorporated the name was changed to honor Major William H. Lewis who had estab-lished Fort Lewis in 1874 near the present location of the city swimming pool. According to Wikipedia, Lewistown hosts two an-nual events: (1) The Chokecherry Festival includes a chokecherry culinary contest, a pit spitting contest, and a 5k run/walk and 10k run. The event has been held for more than twenty-three years. (2) The Metis Celebration is the only celebration for Metis people within the continental U.S. It is traditionally held on Labor Day weekend and includes a powwow, fiddling, jigging, and other Metis related activities. (The Métis Nation is comprised of descendants of people born of relations between Indian women and European men. The initial offspring of these unions were of mixed ancestry. The genesis of a new Indigenous people called the Métis resulted from the subsequent intermarriage of these mixed ancestry individuals. See the proposed Little Shell Reservation in the notes about Great Falls.) The population of present day Lewistown is 5,885.

Lewistown is also home to the Charlie Russell Chew Choo, which is a four and a half hour train ride through the awe-inspiring mountains and prairies of the Judith Basin and central Montana. (A side trip with this specific destination in mind was required for this experience.) Wildlife abounds on this scenic 56-mile round trip journey, with a plentiful supply of antelope, eagles, deer, hawks and coyotes. Add to that a wonderful prime-rib dinner and a blood pressure raising, attempted train robbery (Oops. Sorry, spoiler alert!) and you have a unique and fun Montana experience.

Chippewa Indian Proverb

SOMETIMES I GO ABOUT PITYING MYSELF, AND ALL THE WHILE I AM BEING CARRIED ACROSS THE SKY BY BEAUTIFUL CLOUDS.

"When all the trees have been cut down, when all the animals have been hunted, when all the waters are polluted, when all the air is unsafe to breathe, only then will you discover you cannot eat money."

—*Cree Prophecy*

Rocky Boy** or **Stone Child,**" was an important Chippewa leader who was chief of a band in Montana in the late 19th century and early 20th century. His advocacy for his people helped gain the establishment of what is called Rocky Boy's Indian Reservation in his honor.

The **Rocky Boy's Indian Reservation** (generally referred to as the Rocky Boy Reservation) is on 172 square miles of land, 40 miles from the Canadian border, within the Bears Paw Mountains. It was established by a congressional statute in 1916 and is home to the Chippewa (Ojibwe) and Cree (Nehiyaw) who have combined to become, and refer to themselves as, the Chippewa Cree Tribe. Rocky Boy's was named after Ah-se-ne-win, Chief Stone Man, and evolved from a misinterpretation of the

Chippewa Cree language. (That seems to be a common occurrence, doesn't it?) There are approximately 6,000 enrolled members in the tribe with 3,323 of them living on the reservation.

Towns on the Reservation:

Agency (Rocky Boy's Agency) has a population of 402.

Azure has a population of 400.

Boneau has a population of 354.

Box Elder is headquarters for the tribe. It was established in 1889 and was first called Bremer, the name of an early homesteader. Eventually, it was changed to Box Elder for the nearby creek lined with box elder trees. The population in 2019 was 47, compared to 794 in the 2000 census. Box Elder was split with the new Rocky Boy West that got most of the population.

Parker School has a population of 625.

Rocky Boy West had a population of 890 in 2010.

St. Pierre has a population of 343. St. Pierre is St. Peter in French. Not at all clear if there is any connection to this name.

Sangrey has a population of 351

Seal for the Chippewa Cree Tribe on the Rocky Boy's Reservation

According to Wikipedia: "There are 326 Indian Reservations in the United States. Most of the tribal land base in the United States was set aside by the federal government as Native American Reservations. In California, about half of its reservations are called Rancherías. In New Mexico, most reservations are called Pueblos. In some western states, notably Nevada, there are Native American areas called Indian Colonies. Populations are total census counts and include non-Native American people as well, sometimes making up a majority of the residents. The total population of all of them is 1,043,762." There is a total of 574 Indian tribes in the United States. Almost one half of them are in Alaska, which is interesting because Alaska has only one reservation. California has the most reservations at 121.

Compare this to Montana's seven reservations which house Indians from ten different tribes.

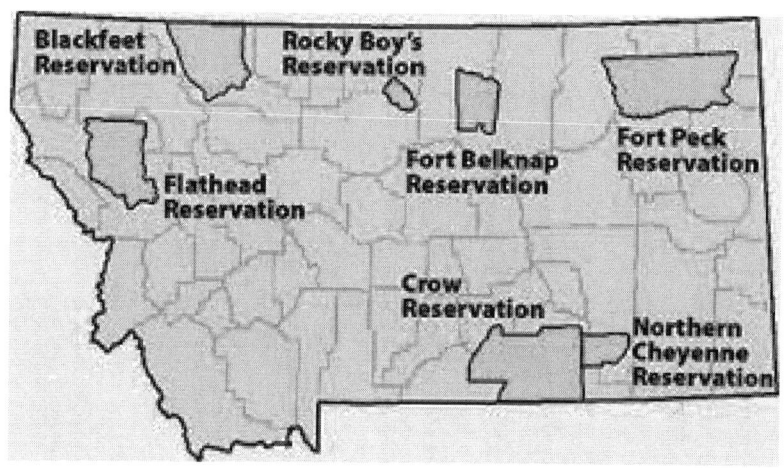

Montana Indian Reservations

Yellowstone National Park was established March 1, 1872, by President Ulysses S. Grant as the first national park in the United States. It is named after the Yellowstone River, the major river running through it. The river gets its name from the Minnetaree Indians, who called it Mi tse a-da-zi, or Yellow Rock River, most likely due to the yellowish formations of the Grand Canyon of the Yellowstone. The Park is a nearly 3,500 square mile wilderness recreation area atop a volcanic hot spot. Mostly in Wyoming, the park spreads into parts of Montana and Idaho. Yellowstone features dramatic canyons, alpine rivers, lush forests, hot springs and gushing geysers, including its most famous, Old Faithful. It's also home to hundreds of animal species, including bears, wolves, bison, elk and antelope. Three of the five entrances to Yellowstone Park are in Montana:

Gardiner is the <u>north</u> entrance, open year-round and brings you to Mammoth Hot Springs. Gardiner was named for Johnston Gardiner, a trapper and mountain man who worked along the Yellowstone River in the 1830's. The town was established in 1872 as an entrance to the park but was not officially founded until 1880. Current population is 879.

Silver Gate is very close to the Wyoming border and is <u>the</u> <u>northeast</u> entrance which puts you at the doorstep of the park's wildlife. Silver Gate is an unincorporated community with a population of 140 people with a definite increase when including summer residents. It gets its name from the nearby Silver Mountain, part of the Beartooth Range, and its location as the "gateway" between mountains.

West Yellowstone is the <u>west</u> entrance to Yellowstone Park, so you can see where it got its name. This entrance brings you to the geysers. The town was founded in 1908 and incorporated in 1966. It's population is 936 with many more people passing through in the summer. West Yellowstone is home to the Grizzly and Wolf Discovery Center which offers the chance to get close to bears and wolves.

Taken on my trip through Yellowstone Park 2/14/2014

(Because all three of the Montana entrances to the Park are close to my home in Billings, I have been through Yellowstone Park many times, starting when I was a young child and most recently on the date of this picture.)

The <u>East</u> Entrance to Yellowstone Park is through Cody, Wyoming, and brings you to Yellowstone Lake, and the <u>South</u> Entrance is outside Jackson Hole, Wyoming.

There are over 60 **Ghost Towns** in Montana, so I will only address those I have seen up close and personal.

Bannack was the original capital of the Montana Territory (1864-1865) with a maximum population of about 10,000. The last of its residents left in the 1970s. It was founded in 1862 and was named for the Bannack Indians who occupied the area before the white man came. The original name was spelled BANNOCK until officially changed in 1898. The town sprang up overnight secondary to the first really big gold strike in Montana on July 28, 1862, by William Eads.

Nevada City is 80 miles from Bannack and is a ghost town that has been turned into a tourist attraction, mainly for its collection of 19th century buildings, 14 of which are original to Nevada City. However, it also provides an impressive collection of "player" (automated) musical instruments, including pianos, organs, violins, brass and woodwinds.

Virginia City is just under 2 miles from Nevada City. Reading from:https://www.visitmt.com/places-to-go/cities-and-towns/virginia-city, "Virginia City was born with the discovery of gold in Alder Gulch in 1863. A boom town of the post Civil War era, Virginia City served as the Montana Territorial Capital for 10 years (1865-1875), until the gold ran out. Both Virginia City and Nevada City have been largely restored and preserved and have become living examples of the real Old West. One hundred fifty buildings have been certified authentic by the Montana Historical Society. Original buildings, dating from the Territorial days, are filled with merchandise and implements used when gold camps flourished in the West. Boardwalks, mechanical music machines, a penny arcade, antique automobiles and even a two-story outhouse add to the Old West atmosphere.

This section of Gold West Country offers many opportunities to relive the adventure of gold rush days. Virginia City's Grand Victorian Ball for Peace 1865 is held in August. Events include a Grand Ball where guests attend in period costume. The Opera House features the Virginia City Players' productions in the style of 19th-century. Virginia City offers the oldest continuously operating summer stock theater west of the Mississippi. You can shop, dine and sleep without leaving the atmosphere of the 1860s." (Which we did!)

The majestic Madison River Valley, just west of Virginia City, features some of the world's finest trout streams, as well as a beautiful mountain backdrop, elevation: 5,882 feet. Originally, Virginia City was named Varina in honor of the wife of Jefferson Davis, president of the Confederacy. However, a local judge, G. G. Bissell, refused to put that name on a legal document. He would "be damned" first, he said. Instead, Mr. Bissell wrote the word Virginia on the top of the document, so that became the town's name, later changed to Virginia City. At its peak the population was about 18,000. According to the 2020 census it was 169.

Montana Ghost Towns

Lewis and Clark Caverns State Park is 55 miles from Virginia City. It is a 3,000-acre public recreation and nature preservation area that includes two visitor centers, ten miles of hiking trails, a campground, and its namesake - limestone caverns. It is claimed that they were discovered in 1882, but there is no substantiation of that. They were first developed for tours around 1900. I went through them when I was in high school – probably about 1956. They are amazing, unbelievable, awesome. Definitely worth seeing, but do it when you are young enough to crawl through small openings and walk over very irregular surfaces. You will learn more about stalagtites (falling from the ceiling of the cave) and stalagmites (rising from the floor of the cave) than you wanted to know.

Lewis and Clark Caverns State Park

"Home is where Montana is
Montana is my home.
From mountain peaks to prairie lands
The places I have known
I am bound to ramble
I am bound to roam
But Home is where Montana is
     (Above line is the one I changed)
Montana is my home."
     Slight paraphrase of lyrics for
     "Home is Where Montana Is"
     by Bruce Anfinson

(This song, being sung by Mr. Anfinson, opens every episode of "The Backroads of Montana," a television show, now in re-runs, highlighting geography, events and people of Montana.)

EPILOGUE — MY NEIGHBORHOOD

If you are a hunter, fisher person, boater, skier –water or snow, hiker, backpacker, camper, mountain climber, gold panner, rock hound (especially if those rocks make beautiful jewelry), bird watcher, wild flower enthusiast, or someone who just likes to be outside in nature, maybe even a history buff, Montana is the place for you. Since I am none of the above, it's hard to understand why I love Montana so much. Explanation? It is home.

Montana issues hunting licenses for the following list of species: antelope, bighorn sheep, bison, black bear, deer, elk, furbearers – for trapping (American badger, bobcat, coyote, ermine, fisher, least weasel, long-tail weasel, lynx, marten, mink, muskrat, North American beaver, North American river otter, raccoon, red fox, striped skunk, and wolverine), migratory birds (coots, ducks, and geese), moose, mountain goat, mountain lion, sand hill crane, swan, turkey, upland game birds (grouse, partridge, pheasant, and turkey), and wolf. It is not at all unusual to see signs on businesses that read: "Closed until I get my Elk" or "Gone Hunting" or "Closed for Hunting Season."

People who are hunters and have the above array of animals from which to pick, want and need guns to accomplish their ends (except, of course, those who hunt with a bow and arrow or a camera). Since Montana is inhabited by many hunters and attracts many more from out of state, guns are prevalent. My father was a hunter, so I grew up used to seeing rifles and shot guns. My former husband was also a hunter and owned guns. I, myself, have never shot a gun and have no interest in doing so, but I am not the norm here in Montana. In fact, guns are so much a part of the culture that the local American Legion baseball teams raise money for their expenses by holding a 30-day raffle for guns: one gun a day for 30 days. It also needs to be mentioned that men are not the only hunters in Montana. My neighbor and his wife hunt together, and she shoots the animals, helps dress them out when they get back home, and finally cooks the resulting meat for their dinners. Also, the last time I was getting my hair cut, the clinician got a text from a friend and showed me the picture which was of an elk her friend, a woman, had just shot. It was a very big, many points buck of which both friends were very proud.

View of Beartooth Mountains from Montana Highway 420 just past the 5-mile marker when coming from Absarokee toward my cabin.

Mountains, the very thing for which Montana was named, they are a plenty. According to Wikipedia, there are 97 mountain ranges listed, not mountains, but mountain ranges, which means a lot more than 97 mountains. Granite Peak, part of the **Beartooth Range of the Northern Rockies,** is the highest point in Montana at a height of 12,799 feet. (The Beartooth Mountain Range, which originates in the Beartooth Wilderness, is the backdrop to my cabin on the Stillwater River.) Granite Peak is definitely on the list of mountains that people choose to climb, but it is not recommended for the novice. Other climbing recommendations are: Mount Siyeh, the fifth tallest peak in Glacier National Park at 10,014 feet; Reynolds Mountain, also in Glacier Park; Beehive Peak, 10,742 feet in Big Sky; the Rimrocks, sandstone rock formations at Billings; the Bozeman Pass, limestone just outside of Bozeman; Hyalite Canyon, ice climbing in

Bozeman; Pollock Mountain and Bishop's Cap, in Glacier Park; Hellgate Gulch, outside of Helena; and Winter Wall, outside of Norris.

Of course, these mountain ranges are not only for climbing and hiking, but also skiing and snowboarding. There are several developed downhill ski areas. Big Sky Resort is an hour south of Bozeman and an hour north of Yellowstone National Park; Whitefish Mountain Resort, also known as Big Mountain, is in the town of Whitefish and borders Glacier National Park; Bridger Bowl Ski Area is just outside of Bozeman; Discovery Ski Area is one hour west of Butte; Montana Snowbowl is just outside of Missoula; Lookout Pass Ski and Recreation Area is on the Montana/Idaho border on Interstate 90; Lost Trail Powder Mountain is near the Montana/Idaho border near Highway 93; Great Divide Ski Area is less than 20 miles from Helena; Snowdown Montana is on Highway 89 out of Neihart; Blacktail Mountain is near the western shore of Flathead Lake; **Red Lodge Mountain** is near the Wyoming border and Yellowstone Park in Red Lodge; and Maverick Mountain is in southwestern Montana within the Beaverhead-Deer Lodge National Forest by Polaris.

There are seven national forests in Montana, all of them inviting hikers, backpackers, campers and outdoors people to come on in, and leave it the way you found it. (1) The Beaverhead-Deer Lodge National Forest, covers eight counties in southwest

Montana, and is the largest national forest in Montana at 3.35 million acres, approximately the size of Connecticut. (2) The **Custer-Gallatin National Forest,** which is the one that encompasses my cabin on the Stillwater River, is spread throughout south central and southeastern Montana and extends into northwest South Dakota. The entire forest is part of the Greater Yellowstone Ecosystem — one of the largest nearly intact ecosystems on Earth. (3) The Bitterroot National Forest is in southwest Montana and extends into Idaho. The iconic Frank Church-River of No Return Wilderness, one of the most extensive wilderness tracts in the country, is encompassed by this forest. (4) The Lolo National Forest is two million acres in western Montana that surround the city of Missoula and extends west to the Idaho border. There are 30 developed campgrounds within the forest area. (5) The Helena-Lewis and Clark National Forest is in central and north central Montana and straddles the Continental Divide. This forest surrounds the Montana State Capital, Helena, and the Gates of the Mountain Wilderness, named by Meriwether Lewis. It also encompasses Great Falls and the Lewis and Clark Interpretive Center, which is a must for people interested in following their footsteps. (6) The Kootenai National Forest is in the far northwest corner of the state, bordered by British Columbia to the north and Idaho to the west. And finally, (7) the Flathead National Forest is just south of Glacier National Park, covers 2.4 million acres, and encompasses the Bob Marshall Wilderness.

Wikipedia, lists about 50 rivers in Montana with another almost 30 categorized as creeks. It would only be a slight exaggeration to say, throw a rock and close to where it lands will be a stream of free flowing water. The longest river by far is the Missouri at 2,340 miles, the Milk River is second at 729 miles and the Yellowstone third at 692 miles. That makes the Yellowstone the longest, free flowing (which means undammed) river in the United States. The Roe River, which runs from Giant Springs to the Missouri River, just outside of Great Falls, holds claim to being the shortest river in the world at 201 feet. The top twelve fly fishing streams as listed on the Internet are: Gallatin, Madison,, Missouri, Yellowstone, Blackfoot, Big Hole, Clark Fork, Bitterroot, Rock Creek, Bighorn, Sun and Smith. Without a question, my second child and oldest son, Mike Campbell, would disagree. He fishes on the **Stillwater River**, that runs by his cabin, which he has owned for 20+ years, and is next door to my cabin, which his sister and I have owned for about two years. He catches fish all the time, has fished on many of those rivers on the list with disappointing results, and speaks very highly of his home river. Game fish commonly found in Montana rivers and creeks are: trout (bull, cutthroat, brown, brook, rainbow), paddlefish, pike, bass, perch, catfish, sturgeon, and burbot.

When I asked Mike to write something for this book, he chose, instead of fly fishing, his second favorite activity of "tubin," and here it is:

"It's a beautiful summer day. The sky is deep blue broken only by the occasional white cumulus clouds moving overhead in a slow and easy progression. The river sparkles in the background. It's early afternoon, and the group of intrepid tubers have gathered for what always turns out to be the highlight of a day that is otherwise filled with liberal expressions of love and laughter.

"I have taken inner tubes down the same stretch of river for over 50 years, since my grandfather built his simply perfect, 6-sided cabin on the bank of the Stillwater River. He was a remarkable man possessed of a warm and welcoming demeanor and a sharp inquisitive mind. He was an inventor and a tinkerer. He built the cabin with his own hands and the help of a few willing familial laborers. And, his cabin is the reason for and the beginning of my love affair with the river. But my grandpa is another story. This is a story about the river and its gifts given to tubers.

"Tubing on the river is a very simple and inexpensive passage to whitewater adventure. The necessary gear consists of a pair of river shoes, and ideally a swimsuit and rash guard, but tennis shoes, shorts and a t-shirt will do just fine. Also, a substantial truck tire inner tube is a must. The plastic blowup variety meant for a swimming pool or placid lake quickly becomes a useless piece of flaccid plastic in this river.

"The group walks up the dirt road around the bend and down to the riverbank. Entry into the water is a slow and careful process. The water is bracingly cold and brilliantly clear. The river moves swiftly over the smooth and slick rocks lining the river bottom. Approach the water too quickly and one misstep leaves you flailing and falling into the icy cold water. If we have beginners in the group there is a pause for instruction in case a tuber becomes separated from their tube: head above water, feet downstream, float in a seated position, paddle toward the bank until you can stand. Let someone else recover the tube and walk the bank to reunite tube and tuber.

"We jump onto the tubes, face down as always. This river demands your full attention and floating on your back with your feet and hands in the air does not allow for the ability to choose your path with the urgency necessary to avoid being turned upside down by any one of the large boulders the river deliberately moves into your path. Face down, head first, paddling swiftly to the middle of the river to catch the deepest water and the fastest currents, white water in our sights. Finding the white water is the goal. Finding the water that flows easily between the exposed boulders and over the submerged ones is the ideal path. At the bend is the first set of rapids, and the ride over the biggest leaves a splash of water in my face and after a head shake and wipe of my brow my head is up and searching for the next rapid. The float continues as I catch the rapids that spray the cold water onto my face and back. The river is lined with cabins on one side, but the other side is lined with willows and cottonwoods leading up a hillside dotted with wildflowers that disappear as the hillside turns into a rocky cliff. The natural scenery is breathtakingly beautiful just as it was when the Absaroka tribe called this land their home.

"The float is a blend of whitewater rapids and gently flowing water over both deep and shallow spots in the river. Those gentler stretches allow for a bit of reflection on the gifts the river has given me and many others over the years. The river provides a deep sense of connection to the earth. Its waters constantly flowing, always present, continuously changing, but still the same. It has provided adventure but also peace and love and togetherness in abundance. It has become such an important part of me that I can close my eyes, wherever I am, and see the crystal-clear water in my mind and feel its cool comforting touch on my skin. The river is in my blood but more profoundly a part of my spirit.

"The tubing run ends in a deep pool perfectly situated and timed in order to set the tubes on the bank and go for a refreshing dip in the perfect Montana stream. The water that was snow only 24 hours earlier welcomes my full body immersion as I catch my breath and count my blessings.

"We gather our tubes and head for the trucks waiting at the bridge. The tubers are soaking wet and chilled from the swim but smiling broadly, each relating their story of the big rapid that sent them reeling or drenched them from head to toe, or both. The satisfaction among the group is palpable. The river connects us to each other, to the land, and to Montana. We arrive back at the cabin and inevitably someone, probably me, says "who wants to go again?"

View of the Stillwater River, as it runs by My Cabin, as taken from the Midnight Canyon Bridge

The **Stillwater River**, which is approximately 70 miles long, rises in the Absaroka-Beartooth Wilderness south of the Beartooth Mountains, converges with Rosebud Creek in Absarokee, and flows into the Yellowstone River just south of Columbus. This is "My" river because the one half acre upon which my cabin sits extends to the half way mark underlying the river. (I don't own the water flowing above, but I do own some of the land over which it flows. Honest I do.)

The **Shirley Cabin,** approximately 100 yards from my cabin on the Stillwater, is the reason I am here and attached to this area of Montana. My father, Eldon Shirley, his father, Ralph Shirley, and my uncle O.M. (Tuffy) Dahl built a cabin. My father purchased an acre in 1958 for $1,000, (Today's value would be about $150,000) designed a one-room, six-sided structure (with the help of his son-in-law Derry Brodsack, an engineering student at Montana State in Bozeman), pre-cut all the siding logs in Billings, brought them to the cabin site in his home-made trailer, and proceeded to construct a structure that is still in use today by the fourth generation of "Shirleys." Another son-in-law, John H. Smith, designed and built the kitchen cabinets, and his third son-in-law, Pat Campbell (my children's father), helped by doing the, not so glamorous but necessary, general labor. The cabin was completed in 1960 and my sisters and I, with our spouses and children, began coming to spend time in it. Many family events were celebrated at that cabin: birthdays, weddings, anniversaries, family reunions and the celebration for my graduation from college. All the years of coming to the Shirley Cabin, with the last twenty including son Mike's cabin, created an attachment to the Stillwater and this area. So, when the cabin next door to Mike's became available, I jumped, so excited and so pleased that it all fell into place.

My number four child and third son, Matt Campbell, has the following to say about his memories of the Shirley Cabin:

"My fondest childhood memories of living in Montana were going to my grandparent's cabin on the Stillwater River. The orange, odd-shaped, hexagonal, cabin seemed out of place in the rugged Montana landscape, but it was a place for joy and love. The cabin offered an experience where I could immerse myself in the simplistic pleasures of being a kid. Swimming in the freezing white water, hopping from boulder to boulder on the river banks, discovering the perfect flat river rock to skip across the water, basking in the warm July days, waiting with unbridled excitement to go on the next tube run, chasing my siblings with the perfect water balloon, and feeding the neighbor's horse carrots as we made sure our fingers were not part of the meal, are all experiences that are part of me. As an adult, I look back with fondness and a deep sense of appreciation toward my grandparents for building a cabin and starting an unbreakable bond with the Stillwater.

"I cherish my memories of swimming, throwing water balloons, and feeding horses. However, a more lasting, more impactful, memory that has transcended my Montana memories, is the first time I paid attention to the beauty and mystery of Midnight

Canyon. I remember standing, as a child, thinking it was the most beautiful thing I had ever seen. Distant, delicately carved from an ancient glacier, providing a gateway for unlimited joys and special memories.

"As an adult, I lost contact with the Stillwater. Going to college, starting a career, marriage, and raising two boys became a priority. The Stillwater roar and Midnight Canyon's gaze became a distant and fond crutch to remind me that I once spent time on the Stillwater.

"Upon returning to the Stillwater, to join the family in celebration of our mother's 80+1 birthday, the bridge, the white water, the boulders, and the roar of the rapids were all familiar. During moments of silence, I would frequently look upriver into Midnight Canyon and be transported back to my childhood. I recalled the warmth, love, and joy of a place, etched and carved into the essence of my being. Reconnecting with an essential and fundamental part of who I am was transformative.

"The Stillwater River and Midnight Canyon replenished my soul. I did not realize my return would reunite me with who I am and bring harmony, a sense of peace, and comfort to my soul. I am part of the Stillwater and Midnight Canyon, taking it with me wherever I go."

"Montana: where the elevation is usually higher than the town's population.."
—Author Unknown

*(There are 226 people in Nye.
I would say the above quotation rings true.)*

The address for my cabin is **Nye**, Montana. Go figure. I am probably equidistant between Nye and Absarokee, but Nye it is. Nye is an unincorporated community that was originally a copper mining camp. The town sprang into existence when Jack Nye and the Hedges brothers staked their claim. Mining continues to be an important part of the area's economy. The Stillwater mine for palladium and platinum is the only such producer in the United States. (Montana is a leader in talc production and is a major producer of copper/molybdenum, garnets, and silver. It also produces bentonite, common clays, construction sand/gravel, crushed/

dimension stone, gold, lime, and gemstones. Just not all of those in Nye.)

Carter's Camp, which seems to be the Nye hub, lies in between the mine and my cabin. It is basically a bar, restaurant and very few, maybe three, motel rooms. According to an article in the Billings Gazette in 2012, Carter's Camp was established 60 years ago by the Grant Smith family. "The familiar wooden building, set strikingly in the shadow of the Beartooth Mountains, has the authentic feeling of the old west. It's a little rough around the edges, as one part-time resident put it. You won't find designer items on the menu, no foie gras or escargot. It's more meat and potatoes offerings..." Current owner, Bruce Austin, was born in Hawaii in 1945, lived in Iowa, Nebraska and Ohio and has moved back to Montana to rescue Carter's Camp. I'm so glad he did. Welcome!

The only other businesses in Nye, down the highway about one half mile from Carter's Camp, are a post office/very small convenience store combination and gas station. Needless to say, I don't spend much time in Nye, even though I live there.

Absarokee – (pronounced **Ab-SORE-kee**) is about 12 miles (seven of them paved and the other five sometimes gravel or just dirt) from my cabin on the Stillwater River that is considered to be in Nye, Montana, and is the town I most closely identify as home. It has a current population of 1,061. Absarokee has a couple of bar/restaurants,two just restaurants, one sit down the other drive up, a post office, a motel with 12 rooms, several hair dressers for people and one groomer for dogs (who is quite wonderful and great with my dogs), a hardware store, a small medical clinic (no doctors on the premises), two banks, a quilt store, AND a grocery store, as well as a half dozen other businesses. Let me just add a note about that grocery store. They have young men who carry the groceries to your car. That in itself is novel and adding to that is the conversation from one of those young men on his way to my car. He said before he got to work that morning he was rounding up cattle since before dawn. I dare you to hear that from a city bag boy. That is, of course, if you can find a bag boy in the city. The delight of small towns!

Absarokee is a small town in south-central Montana that you pass through on your way to somewhere else. (In fact we didn't even pass through it on any of these trips, but I had to include it because it is where I buy groceries.) It rests between Columbus and Red Lodge on Highway 78 at the base of the Beartooth Mountains. The name Absarokee comes from two Hidatsa Indian words: "apsaa" meaning large beaked bird and "lookei" meaning children. Therefore, Absarokee literally means: Children of large beaked birds, referencing the Crow Indian Tribe whose people were the early inhabitants of this area. The name Crow came from the French fur traders who interpreted apsaa lookei to mean "people of the crows." It was Sever T. Simonson who believed it meant "Our People" and ultimately christened the town he founded with that name. It is believed that the difference in spelling between Absarokee and the nearby Absaroka Mountain Range is simply poor penmanship on someone's part.

It wasn't until October of 1892 that the federal government opened up the land around Absarokee for settlement, subsequent to an agreement made with the Crow Indians, through political pressure, that they move to their reservation that had been established by treaties in 1851 and 1868. Mr. Simonson had arrived just prior to that event declaring "squatter's rights" at the confluence of the Stillwater and East Rosebud Rivers. Together with his nephew, Oliver H. Hovda, they built a log hotel, a saloon, a livery stable and blacksmith shop and established a trading post. A post office was included in December of 1892 in Simonson's home, and he served as the first post master. Hovda's home was built by a local rancher, Jacob Wagner, was two stories tall and located on the main street of Absarokee. It became known as the "Big Yellow House" and still is, and is currently on the National Register of Historic Sites.

School House turned Community Center

Another structure of note in Absarokee is the "Cobblestone" building which was the original high school. According to www.HistoricMT.org: "…Although Absarokee's high school district was the smallest in the state, the town had high hopes and great determination. Residents joined forces holding dances, bazaars, and bake sales to raise funds. A $20,000 bond issue was established and the work progressed. With cobbles gathered from nearby fields and riverbeds, the school was built on donated land with volunteer labor. W. R. Plew, an engineer at Montana State University at Bozeman who promoted appropriate designs in rural schools, is credited with the plans. The Cobblestone School was fully accredited with three full-time teachers. The first five students graduated in the spring of 1922. Pupils came from as far away as Limestone (currently a ghost town) and Nye, boarding with local families during the winter months. An outstanding example of a simple school built with locally available materials...Most of its original woodwork and fixtures remain intact...." Over the years the Cobblestone School housed many different levels of schooling, but has been retired and remodeled to become a community meeting center. A new, modern high school was built in Absarokee in 1989 with the first graduating class in 1990.

It so happens that one of the groups that now meets at the re-assigned Cobblestone building is the Stillwater Quilters and Needlecrafters, of which I am a new member. The group was actually started in 1998 as a follow-up to an adult education class in Columbus taught by Agnes Cowan. She and her husband had returned to Montana after periods of time living in California, Texas and Costa Rica, rearing their daughter and retiring from their respective careers. Agnes credits Dorothy Miller (who lived to be 101 years old) with being the driving force behind the group. Dorothy was a skilled quilter with many years of experience, at age 80+, and perfectly capable of helping others learn what she already knew. Over many years the group donated their finished quilts to Lutheran World Relief, most years about 80 quilts, but one particularly productive year the count was 110. The process went something like this: Dorothy put together most of the tops (the patchwork of fabric sewed into patterns); there would be yardage of whole fabric, matching the size of the tops, spread out on tables; and batting, also cut to match the size of the tops and bottoms, would be placed in between so that the ladies could either pin them in place to later be sewn together or tied together with pieces of yarn. The only thing left at that point was to put on the binding, that is sewn around the edges of the entire quilt.

In addition to making extraordinarily beautiful quilts, which they displayed in a quilt show every year, the Stillwater Quilters (name later changed to Stillwater Quilters and Needlecrafters) provided its members with an opportunity to socialize. They would take two or three car loads of women to neighboring towns to shop for materials and go out to lunch and/or dinner. Usually twice a year, spring and fall, they would get together at a nearby resort, Big Timber and Red Lodge were particular favorites, for a three-day retreat. They would bring their sewing machines and all their supplies and check in, to be taken care of by someone else while they worked on their projects and visited with each other. Their top membership was about 30 women.

Many women have come and gone from the Stillwater Quilters and Needlecrafters, but some of the originals remain. Four of them graduated from Absarokee High School, married Montana men within one year of graduation, moved away from Absarokee for at least a couple of years, reared their families, retired from their careers, and moved back to Absarokee. Two of those four are Dorothy's daughters: Doris (Miller) Madison and Georgette (Miller) Scheafer. Doris graduated from high school in 1952 when it was still in the Cobblestone building. When she and her husband moved back home after living in Billings during their working lives, they moved pnto his family's ranch, approximately eight miles outside Absarokee. The ranch has been in his family since 1890, and according to Doris, "Make no mistake. The ranch is very primitive. It has no running water, no plumbing, but does have electricity." They lived there about 20 years and have recently moved into town, into the home in which she grew up, but Doris says her husband goes out to the ranch almost every day. (Since this writing he has passed.) Georgette and her husband became very active in the community upon their return from Oregon. Georgette says: "Our plan all along was to return to Montana as soon as we could," and she was grateful to be at home following his recent death.

The other two of the four are Frances (Yates) Haley and Clara (Oltrogee) Borland. Frances actually lived with her family on their ranch in Fishtail, about six miles southwest of Absarokee, and returned to that family ranch in Fishtail with her computer programmer, not a rancher, husband after living in Colorado for roughly 30 years. When asked what brought them back to Montana, she replied: "I always dreamed that we could." Clara and her husband never really left Absarokee for any length of time, only long enough to finish his military service, plus one year as a patrolman in Alaska. According to Clara, that was long enough to know that they didn't want to raise their family anywhere but home. They were business owners in the community: first taking over his parents' Cobblestone Garage, then building and operating the Cowboy Bar in Fishtail (which is now a restaurant named Montasia, serving Montana and Asian food), Clara had a catering business, Clara started the local quilt shop in partnership with two other women (Georgette Scheafer and Gail Eberhardt), then owning and operating it by herself, and finally they developed the Crow Chief Meadows Subdivision just south of Absarokee from which they have just sold the final of 65 lots. Clara was also very involved in the "save the Cobblestone" project that allowed the original high school building to remain intact and be turned into the community center it is today.

A Bridge to Nowhere!

An interesting aside involving the Doris and Harvey Madison couple is the bridge they purchased when it was up for auction. They bid and paid $400, as they were the only bidder. The bridge was being removed from crossing the Rosebud River on Stillwater Road heading out of Absarokee. The Madisons wanted to put that bridge over the Stillwater River by their home so they could get to their own pastures without taking a circuitous route of some seven miles. However, because of all the governmental red tape that never happened, and the bridge sits in the middle of a pasture today. Testimony to bureaucratic inefficiency.

All of this is by way of demonstrating that when Montana is your home, you want to live in Montana. People who feel they have to leave Montana for whatever reason, begin to look for ways to come back, and with few exceptions they do. Montanans returning to Montana are common among the Montana population. I know. I am one of them. And, I can't resist another small town story. This year I called the woman who does my taxes, only to hear that she is currently in California tending to a sick relative but is still doing taxes. All I need to do is take my documents to the "Water Building" and give them to Judy who will in turn send them to the accountant. So, dutifully, I go to the water building with packet in hand, only to find that Judy is not there, but a gentleman, who I don't know, but then I don't know Judy either, says that he will take my packet and make sure that Judy gets it. I hand him the packet that contains all my personal information, including the oh so protected, social security number, and walk away without a backward glance, until I'm driving home. All I could think was, only in small town America could something like that happen. And, it all went well, with no problems.

Towns between Absarokee and Red Lodge on Highway 78:

Fishtail is an unincorporated community established in 1901 and named after a Mr. Fishtail who lived in the area. It has a general store, gas station, antique and gift shop, bar and restaurant. Population is 512.

Roscoe is an unincorporated community with a population of 49 people. It was established in 1901 under the name of Morris with a Mrs. Morris as the postmistress. However, because there was another town in Montana named Morris she was asked to pick a new name and in 1905 it was re-christened Roscoe. That was the name of her favorite horse. Roscoe's claim to fame is the Grizzly Bar and Grill, in which I have eaten many times. My oldest son's rehearsal dinner, the night before his wedding at the Shirley Cabin on the Stillwater River, was held there.

Red Lodge is 54 miles from my cabin on the Stillwater River that is considered to be in Nye, Montana. It is a thriving small town, population 2,257. There are many stories explaining where the name came from: (1) the Crow Indians painted their lodges with a red clay found in the area, (2) John Webber, an early pioneer, said it was simply because there were so many lodges of "red" men in the area, and (3) there is a huge outcropping of mineral bearing rock with a red hue on the side of a mountain west of Red Lodge, out of which flows a large stream of water. When seen from a distance of 10-12 miles it resembles remarkably an Indian teepee/lodge. Red Lodge is a destination town, providing the touristy, arty amenities that people enjoy. In addition to all the normal services you would expect to find, plus a 10-bed hospital and medical clinic, it has a plethora of restaurants that serve very good food, and unique retail shops, including an old fashioned candy store. The town is located at the base of the Beartooth Highway, which leads to the Silver Gate entrance to Yellowstone National Park, and Red Lodge Mountain provides snowboarding and snow skiing activities throughout the winter. Therefore, the town has year around appeal. This is not a town that I visit frequently, but it is in my neighborhood and provides a venue for special occasions.

Columbus (already mentioned in Western Montana Section, just a little more here) is found going the other direction on Highway 78 where 78 meets Interstate 90 beside the Yellowstone River. It has all the services available in Absarokee plus two gasoline stations, a florist that offers a variety of candies along with the beautiful flowers, a Family Dollar Store, a McDonalds and a small, six-bed hospital and medical clinic with physicians on staff. Oh, and the Bearstone Café (name is a combination of <u>Bear</u>tooth Mountains and Yellow<u>stone</u> River) which is the one owned by my youngest daughter, Kori Campbell, and her husband, Matt Eubank. Before I let her speak I want to introject that every year in the backyard of their home the same female deer gives birth. One of those years I was there within hours of that birth. The mother had left the newborn in the yard while she went to the river for a drink. What a sight. Tiny little fawn curled up in a ball, absolutely motionless, to the point that I was concerned if it was alive, awaiting his mother's return. (It was a brand new baby boy.)

Here's Kori: "Although I was born in Billings and lived there until the middle of the second grade, at Fratt Memorial School, I grew up in California with the rest of my siblings. When my mother moved to Big Fork, Montana, in the early 1990's, I moved with her just to see how I would like it. Obviously, I liked it because I ended up living in the area for almost eight years, even after my mother left. During the time I was living with her in Big Fork, I worked as a waitress at the Big Fork Inn and Echo Lake Cafe, both of which have been around for a very long time, and Show Time, which was a brand new restaurant. I then moved to Whitefish and worked as a waitress at Moose's on the Mountain and Rocco's in Kalispell. While I was managing Rocco's my younger brother, Mason, came to work there as a host, which was an interesting experience for us both. Also, during that time I would go with my friend, Laura, to hike in Glacier Park. What sticks out in my memory are the comments overheard from tourists visiting the park: 'Do the fish freeze in place in the winter?' 'Where do they keep the animals during the winter?' 'What time do they turn off the waterfalls?' After several years I moved to Lakeside and went to work as a waitress at the Montana Grill, later moving to Missoula where I did the books, tended bar and filled in waitressing at The Depot. All of these were well known, popular restaurants and bars. After moving back to California, I met my husband, Matt Eubank, moved with him to Arizona, and got married **in** the Stillwater River alongside both my brother Mike's cabin and the Shirley Family Cabin. While in Montana for the wedding my new husband was offered the opportunity to take over a sprinkler business from one of the Midnight Canyon residents. He did and we moved to Columbus where we now own and operate the Bearstone Café. There was a couple, Kaydel and Randy, I used to serve every Friday night when I worked at Rocco's in Kalispell. They had two small children. They moved to a ranch outside of Columbus about five years ago and now frequent the Bearstone and keep me updated on their college age children. That is the small town Montana that I love." (Another change since this writing: The Bearstone Café is no longer in business, a victim of the inability to find people who want to work.)

Just off Interstate 90 in Columbus

Yet another small town story: my daughter-in-law called the florist, Chris in Columbus, to order a bouquet of pink flowers sent to me. The florist said, "Are you sure you want them to be pink? Her favorite color is red. She has a red car and plants red geraniums every year." And yet another, same florist, only this time in response to an order from my daughter who had asked that the flowers be delivered that same day, to which she was told, "Well, she's not at home. When I drove by there I didn't see her car."

Towns between Columbus and Billings on Interstate 90:

Park City was known as Young's Point in 1882 when settlers from Ripon, Wisconsin, came in boats on the Yellowstone River. The settlers planted trees to make it look like a park. When the railroad came they wanted to name the town Rimrock, for the cliffs to the north, but the settlers insisted on Park City. In retaliation for their stubbornness, the railroad general manager moved his railroad yards to the neighboring town of Laurel. Population of Park City is 813.

Laurel is a major railroad town. The Northern Pacific, Great Northern, Chicago, Burlington and Quincy Railroads all go/have gone through there. Once again (as with Red Lodge) there are many opinions as to where the name came from. (1) It was named by a railroad man for a member of his family. (2) It was named by a railroad man for his home town of Laurel, Mississippi. (3) It was originally named Carlton, and nobody has any idea why it was changed. And finally, (4) it was named for the laurel plant, but none of them grow in the area so that explanation is questionable. The post office opened in 1886. Laurel is a full service town with everything except a hospital, probably because it's so close to Billings (16 miles). Population is 6,834. (My sister and her family lived in Laurel for about 35 years, so although I didn't ever live there, I got to know it somewhat.)

Billings is about 68 miles from my cabin on the Stillwater River considered to be in Nye, Montana.

Billings, as has already been stated, is the largest town in Montana and the town in which I was born and grew up. If you can't find what you are looking for In Billings, you don't need it. It is home to not one but two full service hospitals. SCL Health, formerly St. Vincent's Hospital, has 222 beds, and Billings Clinic, formerly Deaconess Hospital, has 304 beds. Billings has become a major medical center between Minneapolis and Seattle and Denver. The city is named for Frederick H. Billings, a former president of the Northern Pacific Railroad from Woodstock, Vermont. According to Wikipedia: "The Crow people, who are indigenous to the area, call the city *Ammalapáshkuua*. It means 'where they cut wood', and is named as such because of a sawmill built in the area by early white settlers. The Cheyenne name is *É'êxováhtóva*, 'sawing place' and the Gros Ventre name is *óhuutébi n nh*, 'where they saw lumber,' both also named for the sawmill, or translations of the Crow name.

William Clark (of the Lewis and Clark Expedition) passed through the Billings area on July 25, 1806, He arrived at what is now known as Pompeys Pillar and wrote in his journal '... at 4 P M arrived at a remarkable rock ... this rock I ascended and from its top had a most extensive view in every direction.' Clark carved his name and the date into the rock, leaving the only remaining physical evidence of their expedition. He named the place Pompy's Tower, naming it after the son of his Shoshone interpreter and guide, Sacajawea. In 1965, Pompeys Pillar was designated as a national historic landmark, and was proclaimed a national monument in January 2001.

The area where Billings is today was known as Clark's Fork Bottom. In 1877, settlers from the Gallatin Valley area of the Montana Territory formed Coulson, the first town of the Yellowstone Valley. The town was started when John Alderson built a sawmill and convinced P. W. McAdow to open a general store and trading post on land Alderson owned on the bank of the Yellowstone River. Coulson was a rough town of dance halls and saloons and not a single church. The town needed a sheriff and the famous mountain man John 'Liver-Eating' Johnson took the job. Many disagreements were settled with a gun in the coarse Wild West town. Soon a graveyard was needed and Boothill Cemetery was created. It was called Boothill because most of the people in it were said to have died with their boots on. Today, Boothill Cemetery sits within Billings' city limits and is the only remaining physical evidence of Coulson's existence. When the railroad came to the area it had two sections side-by-side, about two miles west of Coulson. Being able to make far more money by creating a new town on these two sections the railroad decided to create the new town of Billings, the two towns existed side by side for a short time with even a trolley running between them. However, most of Coulson's residents moved to the new booming town of Billings. In the end, Coulson faded away with the last remains of the town disappearing in the 1930s. Today Coulson Park, a Billings city park, sits on the river bank where the town of Coulson once was.

Needless to say, I have many memories of, stories about and connections to Billings, having lived there through my childhood and early adulthood, including:

Family of Origin – parents, sister, grandparents, aunts and uncles, all to be found now in the Sunset Memorial Gardens Cemetery.

Streets I lived on – Miles Avenue, Poly Drive, Lewis Avenue, Arvin Road, and Spruce Street.

Schools I attended – Rimrock Elementary – 2nd through 4th grades (no longer there), McKinley Elementary – 5th Grade (recently remodeled and still being used for elementary school), Jefferson – 6th Grade (no longer used for classes, but the auditorium was refurbished and is currently used for local stage productions), Lincoln Junior High – 7th through 9th grades (no longer a school but houses the School District 2 Administrative Offices), Billings Senior High School – 10th through 12th grades, (has been added on to and refurbished but continues to function well as one of the three public high schools in Billings) and Eastern Montana College of Education – for maybe a quarters worth of credits (now Montana State University at Billings as noted in the Missoula information.)

Billings Senior High School

As an aside to my high school years, I feel it's imperative that I include the unofficial fight song for Billings Senior High, which was actually outlawed by school administration but was still sung at any and every opportunity – mostly parties and reunions. Here are the words, sing to the melody of the Notre Dame fight song:

Beer, Beer for Old Billings High
Shake up the cocktails, Bring on the Rye
Send some freshmen out for gin

And don't let a sober person in.

We never stagger. We never fall.

We sober up on wood alcohol,

While our loyal faculty

Lies drunk on the barroom floor.

Set 'em up, set 'em up

Win, Win for Billings tonight.

We want to win so go in and fight.

Send the losers home in shame

And add some more glory to our name.

We never stagger. We never fall.

Old Billings High will win over all

V – I – C – T – O – R -Y

Spells victory for Billings High.

Marriage (at St. Patrick's Church, now St. Patrick's Co-Cathedral) and family – husband of 30 years (now divorced), two daughters and four sons, four of the six born in Billings, and all of them growing up there. The oldest going all the way through high school graduating from Billings Central.

Friends and more friends – many of them already passed but a handful remaining and all very special.

Here comes one more small town story: On one of my trips back to Billings, staying at my mother's home on Lewis Avenue,

I answered the door to find a man who was campaigning to be re-seated in the Montana Legislature. Upon hearing his name I was aware that I had graduated from high school between him and his older brother. Small world. You could live in California for a lifetime and never meet anyone from the legislature, let alone one at your front door. Actually, this is the place for the final, no more, small state story: When I was going to graduate school at Colorado State University in 1995-97, I was writing a paper on something (long since forgotten), but I needed information that I thought I could get by talking to someone at the Montana State Capital. I picked up the phone and dialed the number that was published for The Capital. To my absolute shock, the voice on the phone was saying, "Hello, this is Governor Racicot" (pronounced Roscoe). That's right, the governor of the State of Montana actually answered the phone, and as I remember it, he actually answered my question also.

I can't drive down a street in Billings without remembering who lived in what house or what activity took place in what building or the history of the neighborhood or facility. Likewise, conversations with people are often an exercise of following the "yellow brick road" to find who we know in common and not seldom the history associated with those people. (Sure, I remember her and her first husband and her children and who they married, etc.)

I feel very privileged to have Billings as the main pillar of my neighborhood at this time in my life. It feels full circle to me. Whether or not this is where my story ends, it is invaluable to me that as the end approaches I am home. And, I am home when I can still appreciate it, even celebrate it.

My eldest child and number one daughter, Kellie Campbell-Cozart, who shares ownership of this cabin with me has the following to say: "I was born and grew up in Billings, graduated from Billings Central High School. I married at St. Patrick's Church and had my two children, Jason and Jenna, at St. Vincent's Hospital. From age 8 to 15 I swam competitively on the YMCA Swim Team. That meant being in the water at six in the morning, and going from there to school, wet head and all. For any competition we had to travel to other towns in Montana, and for bigger events to North and South Dakota, and Colorado for the Junior Olympics. If my parents didn't go to any particular meet, we car pooled with other parents or, on rare occasions, took a bus, and stayed in the homes of the team members against whom we were competing. Aside from the hard work and commitment that was involved, it was a great way to meet people, make friends, learn some of life's lessons, and experience the state in which I lived. Since I have lived in California for almost 40 years now, I often think of those times and my attachment to Montana. It was a great place to get started, but I doubt that I could go back to those winters. I love having the cabin to go to in the spring and the summer and the fall. And, I love getting to the cabin by traveling through West Yellowstone and down the Gallatin to Bozeman. When I retire there will be much more of that."

My Cabin on the Stillwater River
considered to be in Nye, Montana.

I just can't resist adding this bit of **Montana Trivia.**

1. Montana has more bookstores, birdwatchers, firearms, people who hunt, and people who fish per capita than any other state.

2. Montana is larger than Japan, the United Kingdom, and Italy. If Montana were to secede from the union (and there have been numerous calls to do so) it would be the 62nd largest country in the world.

3. A Montana Yogo Sapphire is the only North American gem included in the Crown Jewels of England.

4. By law it is a felony in Montana for a wife to open her husband's mail.

5. Montana is the only state bordering three Canadian provinces; Saskatchewan, Alberta, and British Columbia.

6. When Great Falls High School was built in 1896, a herd of sheep was used to compact earth around the foundation.

7. Jordan, Montana, the county seat for Garfield County, is 175 miles from the nearest airport, 85 miles from the nearest bus line, and 115 miles from the nearest train.

8. It is perfectly legal in Montana to ride your horse home if you are drunk.

9. Montana is the only state to allow double proxy weddings. In other words, both the bride and groom can have stand-ins exchange matrimonial vows on their behalf. Double proxy divorces, unfortunately, do not exist.

10. Montana is the only state with rivers that drain into three different oceans; the Pacific Ocean, Atlantic Ocean, and Arctic Ocean (by virtue of its drainage into Canada's Hudson Bay).

11. An earthquake in 1959 caused Hebgen Lake in Gallatin County, Montana to recede 22 feet, leaving a wide gravel beach along its lakefront.

12. In 1903 the library in Bozeman, Montana was intentionally built across the street from the city's red-light district and opium dens.

13. Montana is the only state in the U.S. that does not have any statewide ban on texting behind the wheel. No laws against distracted driving.

14. The Montana state constitution mandates that all students must learn American Indian history, culture, and heritage.

15. A cowboy once insisted on riding his horse to his room in the Grand Union Hotel in Fort Benton, Montana. When the manager objected, the two exchanged gunfire. The cowboy was killed before he and his horse made it to the top of the stairs. Fourteen slugs were later removed from his body.

16. A Gideon bible was first placed inside a hotel room in Montana.

17. The bed of bison bones at First Peoples Buffalo Jump State Park in Montana is 13 feet deep.

18. Fort Peck Dam is the largest earth-filled dam in the world and a photo of it was the first photo to grace the cover of Life magazine on November 23, 1936.

19. It is illegal to operate a vehicle with ice picks attached to the wheels within the city limits of Whitehall, Montana.

20. 46 out of Montana's 56 counties are still considered "frontier counties" with fewer than 6 residents per square mile.

21. Mary Fields, who was born into slavery in 1832 and who would later became known as "Stagecoach Mary," was one of the toughest women in the Montana Territory. She was described as a "tart-tongued, gun-toting, hard-drinking, cigar-and-pipe smoking, 6 foot tall, 200 pound black woman who was tough enough to take on any two men." She arrived in Montana to help establish mission schools on the Cheyenne, Crow, Blackfoot and Fort Belknap Indian Reservations.

22 Montana permits urinating along the side of the road (as long as he or she attempts to be modest and does not bother anyone else in the process).

23. Montana has more one-room schools–around 60–than any other state in the country. This is down from 2,600 at its peak.

24. Montana has more than 28,000 family farms and ranches covering 64 percent of the state's land mass.

25. In 1993 the town of Ismay, Montana unofficially changed its name to Joe, Montana as part of a well-organized publicity stunt by the Kansas City Chiefs to honor quarterback Joe Montana.

26. The only place where you can cross the Canada-United States border without having to show any form of ID or

documentation is when you are on a cruise from Waterton, Alberta to Goat Haunt, Montana on Waterton Lake.

27. Cattle rustling in Montana is still punishable by hanging.

28. There are 77 mountain ranges in Montana and 2,991 mountain peaks with names...none of which are among the 50 tallest in the United States.

29. During a smallpox epidemic in the early 1800s two Crow Indian boys rode a white horse over a cliff to sacrifice their lives to save their tribe from the disease. The exact location of that cliff is believed to be along the Yellowstone River near Billings, Montana.

30. According to the folklore of the Crow Nation, the Little People of Montana's Pryor Mountains were dwarves so violent and fearsome they could tear the heart out of an enemy's horse.

31. Montana was the first state to elect a woman (Jeanette Rankin) to Congress in 1916, four years before the 19th amendment gave women the right to vote.

32. The Roe River near Great Falls, Montana is only 201 feet long and is considered the world's shortest river.

33. In 1960 late Senator Ted Kennedy rode a bucking bronco named Skyrocket at a rodeo in Miles City, Montana while stumping for his brother John for President.

34. It is illegal in Montana for a married women to go fishing alone on Sundays. It is also illegal for unmarried women to fish alone at all.

35. Celebrities who call Montana home (at least part of the year) include Michael Keaton (Big Timber), David Letterman (Choteau), Huey Lewis (Stevensville), Howie Long (Flathead Lake), John Mayer (BozemanLivingston), Tom Brokaw (Livingston), and Phil Jackson (Flathead Lake). In addition the following have homes in the Yellowstone Club at Big Sky: Ben Affleck, Justin Timberlake, Dan Quayle, Bill Gates, Jack Kemp, Tom Brady, and Jeff Bridges.

36. Montana has fewer acres of wetlands than any other state.

37. Montana has almost three times as many cows than it has people.

38. Thomas Francis Meagher was an Irish revolutionary convicted of treason and exiled to a penal colony in Tasmania before he served as Montana's territorial secretary and governor.

39. Nearly one fourth of Montana–22.4 million acres–is forested. And the most common tree in the state of Montana is the Ponderosa pine, which was formally adopted as the state tree in 1949 at the urging of the Montana Federation of Garden Clubs.

40. In 1867 the United States Congress annulled all legislation passed by the second and third assemblies of the Montana territory; an unprecedented act in American history.

41. Montana was the first state to adopt a State Lullaby.

42. Montana has more species of mammals (108) than any other U.S. state.

43. Montana was the last state to establish an age limit for buying cigarettes.

44. The first federal census in 1870 showed only 20,595 people living in the Montana Territory.

45. The population of Petroleum County, Montana is just 453 people despite being larger than the state of Rhode Island.

46. Before being named the Montana Territory, Congress considered naming the state "Shoshone" to honor the Indians who lived in the state and "Jefferson" to honor the former President who commissioned the Lewis and Clark Expedition.

47. For over 100 years no one knew the name of the person who sculpted the bronze sculpture of a woman that sits atop Montana's Capitol dome or where it came from. (Belgian-born sculptor Edward Van Landeghem (1865-1955) who named it Montana and said it was his favorite work.)

48. Roy, Montana (pop. 138) owes its name to a spelling mistake. When Walter H. Peck established a post office on his ranch in 1892 he requested the name Ray in honor of a relative. However, someone in Washington D.C. misread the application and returned it with the name Roy instead.